W9-DCJ-268

The Key to the
KINGDOM

David P. Sanzo

The kingdom of God still speaks
of power.

David Sanzo

The Key to the Kingdom
by David Sanzo

Copyright ©1997 David Sanzo
All rights reserved. This book is protected under the copyright laws of the United States of America. This book may not be copied or reprinted for commercial gain or profit. The use of short quotations or occasional page copying for personal or group study is permitted and encouraged. Permission will be granted upon request. Unless otherwise identified, Scripture quotations are from the King James Version of the Bible. Scripture quotations identified NKJV are taken from the *New King James Version of the Bible*: ©1982 by Thomas Nelson, Inc., Nashville, TN.

ISBN 1-56043-249-7
For Worldwide Distribution
Printed in the U.S.A.

Companion Press
An Imprint of Genesis Communications, Inc.
P.O. Box 91011 • Mobile, AL 36691
(334) 607-9191 • (888) 670-7463
Fax (334) 607-0885
Email: GenesisCom@aol.com

ACKNOWLEDGMENTS

I would like to thank the following people for helping me with my book, by allowing me access to their computer when mine was not available: Paul Bennett and New Hope Christian School; Huss and Charles Shearer and Apostolic Lighthouse; Peggy Sims; Marvin Belt; Ron Bridges; Dr. Jimmy Pence; Vic and Kit Mernick; Jerry and Paul Conner and Faith Tabernacle Church, and Sister Lobello, especially for sacrificing her time at work; Alan Willis. Thanks also to Matt Allagas for his help on my computer. Thank you much.

FOREWORD

Every believer is given the glorious privilege of overcoming their enemy and joining in the triumph of Jesus Christ. Unfortunately, too many are taken captive by the cares of this life and never enjoy the honor that all saints possess. Even though God's Word is spoken to their hearts, time and time again, in church service after church service, they never seem to learn the connection between victory and their words.

Therefore, with an undisciplined tongue they talk their way into defeat and thereby become easy prey to the devil—snared by their own words. If they only could learn, not just the power of God's Word, but the power of their own words.

David Sanzo, in this excellent exposé, *The Key to the Kingdom,* reveals to us how our words affect our ability to rule in the spirit. Although the ultimate kingdom of Christ will not be established until He returns in His second coming, we have permission, today, to put on display the victory of the Lord Jesus Christ.

It can not and will not happen until we discipline our speech, conforming it to the principles of God's Word. Sanzo shows us how.

To be sure, our words are a direct revelation of our spirit. If our words are to be changed and become effective in accomplishing God's purpose, then our spirit must be changed.

The world with its evil system needs a changed church whose tongue is like the pen of a ready writer—ready to dip into the ink of the word of God, and with it, write our victory into existence. Whether we need to use words of praise, thanksgiving, or simply learn when to keep silent, let's do so with faith that God will always confirm the word of those who obey His commands. We can be taught how to control our tongue, if we are willing to submit ourselves to the Holy Ghost.

I commend this book to you as a soldier's handbook to guide you, as you seek to champion the cause of Christ, through spiritual warfare, and consequently, to rule in the spirit.

Brian Kinsey
International Speaker

TABLE OF CONTENTS

INTRODUCTION

God has called the Church to exercise the authority and power of God. The Apostle Paul told us that we are to be "strong in the Lord and in the power of his might" (Ephesians 6:10). That means we are to be strong in demonstrating the ability and power of God, in and through our lives.

Jesus spent much of his ministry preaching, teaching, and showing the things of the kingdom of God. We understand that the kingdom of God does not have to do simply with teaching a doctrine or a moral code; it includes the demonstration of the great power of God. Paul told the Thessalonians,

> *For our gospel did not come to you in word only, but also in power, and in the Holy Spirit* (I Thessalonians 1:5).

He also wrote that "the kingdom of God *is* not in word but in power" (I Corinthians 4:20). The kingdom of God comes in supernatural displays of God's abilities and glory.

In fact, if the gospel is not accompanied by the power of God, we have not fully preached the gospel. Paul told the Romans that Christ worked in him to make the Gentiles obedient to the faith by word and deed,

> *Through mighty signs and wonders, by the power of the spirit of God; so that....I have fully preached the gospel of Christ* (Romans 15:18-19).

Of course, His kingdom is not of this world (John 18:36), but is a spiritual kingdom.

John wrote that Jesus has "made us kings and priests unto God and His Father" (Revelations 1:6). Since it is the will of God that we, as the sons of God, would reign in His kingdom, therefore it is the will of God that we reign in the Spirit; we were designed to demonstrate the power of God supernaturally as the sons of God. We are to be "imitators of God" and God is, by definition, supernatural.

In order to reign in the spirit, exercising power and authority in the kingdom of God, we must carefully rein in (control or direct as if with reins) what we speak, for our words carry spiritual power. If we speak the Word of God from our spirit, the power of the Word of God will be released, and the truth will make us free.

We need to keep our spirits pure by laying aside all encumbrances of sin and the distractions caused by the cares of this world. Our words are a key to accomplishing this, "for out of the abundance of the heart, the mouth speaks" (Matthew 12:34, NKJV). Then we shall see God move in power in our lives and the lives of those around us: "Blessed are the pure in heart, for they shall see God" (Matthew 5:8).

Therefore we need: the right heart—Jesus' heart of love; the right spirit—the Holy Spirit; and the right power—the power of the Almighty, to guide our words and actions, our entire lives, to the fullness of life, both now and in eternity, which is found only in God Himself.

If we take care to keep a right heart with God, as David, we will reach spiritual maturity, for God's Spirit will work in us. Then we will speak the Word of the Lord, and blessings of life will flow from our mouths to others, blessing all hearers, including ourselves.

The goal of our being a child of God is to imitate Jesus, who spoke "the words of eternal life" (John 6:68). His words cause us to love Him alone, and teach us to reign in the spirit. Jesus gave us the right to use the authority and the power of the demonstrated ability of God as it is released in the kingdom of God. He said,

> *I will give unto thee the keys of the kingdom of heaven; whatsoever thou shalt bind on earth* [the natural world, the present world] *shall be bound in heaven* [the spiritual world] *and whatsoever thou shalt loose on earth shall be loosed in heaven* (Matthew 16:19).

We bind or loose things in our world by the words we speak. Our words are a key to the uninhibited flow of the power of God in our lives, and in the lives of those around us. When we understand the relationship between our words and the spiritual world, we will line up our words (and thus our spirit) with the will of God. This spiritual alignment causes us to speak His words with the power of His Spirit behind them. When we speak His words in faith, we release the power of His Spirit to bring about the kingdom on earth.

Jesus taught us to pray that the kingdom of God would come. With the words of the Lord's Prayer, we say with our spirit, "Thy kingdom come." May we bring about Thy will on earth, in and through our lives, as it is in heaven (Matthew 6:10). "For Thine is the kingdom, and the power, and the glory, forever" (Matthew 6:13).

I encourage you to look up the scriptures that are referred to but not quoted, and to read the book through twice.

David Sanzo
1997

DEDICATION

I would like to dedicate this book to my brothers and my sister:

John, Phillip, Anna, and Samuel.

I love you. You mean the world to me.

May you know the Jesus I know, the way I know Him,

and so learn to love Him the way I do.

And may it last a lifetime.

CHAPTER ONE
THE DOOR TO THE KINGDOM

The Spiritual World Around Us

During our pilgrimage of faith in this life, we come to realize that there is an entirely different, self-contained world around us—the dimension of the spirit. This spiritual perception comes into focus sometimes gradually, other times suddenly.

It is not a quirk of science fiction. It is not the creation of a novel. It is not the invention of a man-made religion. If we allow God's revelation, the Scriptures, to guide us, we will understand that there are "other beings" beside our human spirits—angels and demons, good and evil spirits—in this spirit realm. God originally designed the two worlds (the natural and the spiritual) to work together.

Many people, even without the benefit or discernment of the Holy Spirit, come to learn that this spirit world is not inaccessible. Following certain laws, people find that they can tap into it, availing themselves of its power. As a result, witches, followers of various religions, psychics, and even some "positive mental attitude" people have tapped into spiritual power in one aspect or another. Not having been led by the Spirit of God, they have used the wrong spirits and have accessed the supernatural. Therefore their dabblings have been destructive to themselves and others. Nevertheless, they have tapped into the spiritual world, a power beyond themselves.

Our interaction with the invisible world will produce blessings or curses, depending on which side we choose. Unless we gain dominion in the spirit, this other world can be dangerous to us, leading into bondage, bodily death, and finally spiritual death. Thus, we absolutely need the Holy Spirit to lead us into all truth (John 14:26), so that the truth will make us free (John 8:32). John the apostle wrote concerning the necessity of truth for our lives, especially in our relation to the spiritual realm:

For I rejoiced greatly when the brethren came and testified of the truth that is in you, just as you walk in the truth. I have no greater joy than to hear that my children walk in truth (III John 3-4, NKJV).

1

Prophets, and other great men and women of faith, have also tapped into the spiritual world, doing so in God's way. God's entrance is by Jesus Christ. Jesus said,

> ...I am the door of the sheep. If anyone enters by Me, he will be saved, and will go in and out and find pasture (John 10:7,9, NKJV).

There are other ways to access the spiritual world but Jesus said,

> ...he who does not enter the sheepfold by the door, but climbs up some other way, the same is a thief and a robber (John 10:1, NKJV).

To be able to enter through God's entrance, we must follow His instructions. Jesus said,

> ...unless one is born of water and the Spirit, he cannot enter the kingdom of God (John 3:5, NKJV).

For us to be able to enter into the sheepfold by the Door, we must be born both of water and of the Spirit.

> ...Repent, and let every one of you be baptized in the name of Jesus Christ for the remission of sins; and you shall receive the gift of the Holy Spirit (Acts 2:38, NKJV).

Jesus' words made the way ever clearer, reaffirming the spiritual nature of God's kingdom:

> My kingdom is not of this world...But now my kingdom is not from here (John 18:36, NKJV).

His kingdom is not of this world. Therefore, it cannot be contacted here by fleshly means. This teaching was (and still is) difficult to understand. That is why, even after His death, Jesus had to appear to the apostles over a period of forty days, speaking to them about the kingdom of God (Acts 1:3).

> Therefore when they had come together, they asked him, saying "Lord, will you at this time restore the kingdom to Israel?" And He said to them: "It is not for you to know the times or seasons which the Father has put in his own

authority. But you will receive power when the Holy Spirit comes upon you; and you will be witnesses to me in Jerusalem, and in all Judea and Samaria, and to the end of the earth" (Acts 1:6-8, NKJV).

He had to continually direct their thinking and aspirations from the horizontal to the vertical. He noted that they were powerless to approach the kingdom of God by themselves, in their own manner and ways of thinking. In the Holy Spirit, Jesus' disciples found the power they were looking for, and the ability to learn and live His truth, displaying His power. Being led by the Spirit, the apostles brought tremendous blessings upon themselves and others.

In order for others to recognize the kingdom of God, power needs to be related to, and reside in, truth. *Truth* informs, and wisdom directs *God's power*, just as, in an opposing sense, *falsehood* directs *evil power*. Jesus explained the incomprehensible to Pilate:

You say rightly that I am a king. For this reason I was born, and for this cause I have come into the world, that I should bear witness to the truth. Everyone who is of the truth hears My voice (John 18:37, NKJV).

Pilate could only respond incredulously, "What is truth?" (v.38). Jesus had a similar message for the "children of Abraham," who were equally dumbfounded:

If you abide in My word, you are My disciples indeed. And you shall know the truth, and the truth shall make you free (John 8:31-32, NKJV).

Jesus' kingdom does include sound doctrine and a moral code, but Jesus is primarily referring here to the release of God's power in believers' lives, which ought to accompany the reception of His Word. Paul told us that the kingdom of God consists in power directed by God's Word—not by mere talk:

But I will come to you shortly, if the Lord wills, and I will know, not the word of those who are puffed up, but the power. For the kingdom of God is not in word but in power (I Corinthians 4:19-20, NKJV).

The kingdom—the exercise of His authority and power—is far removed from vain human imaginings, and it cannot be brought about through works of the flesh. Power comes by proclaiming and implementing His truth. When Jesus says "the truth shall make you free"

(John 8:32), He means that the power of God will move in dramatic fashion, ushering in the kingdom of God:

> And he said unto them, "Verily I say unto you, That there be some of them that stand here, which shall not taste of death, till they have seen the kingdom of God come with power" (Mark 9:1).

The Holy Spirit, by leading us into all truth, draws us into the kingdom of God—the power of God working to bring salvation to lost souls, accomplishing the truly miraculous, and gaining the victory over the power of sin. The kingdom of God is a matter of "righteousness, and peace, and joy in the Holy Ghost" (Romans 14:17). We are called to enter an Apostolic realm where God reigns through us.

The kingdom of God releases all of God's blessings to us. These include spiritual blessings, physical blessings, mental blessings, social blessings, and even financial ones. The kingdom of God will release to us the abundant life that Jesus talked about. The phrase "abundant life" means that, not only will we experience fantastic living in the eternal future, but that we will discover how truly outstanding our present life can be as well. It is to dwell in a level of life far beyond the mundane, sharing in God's divine life.

This was certainly the case in the healing of Peter's mother-in-law. When Jesus touched her, "she arose," and served him (Matthew 8:14-15). God blesses—touches us with his resurrection power—so we can serve Him. He gives us abundant life, true prosperity of the spirit. He also prospers us in mind and body. For it is the will of God, not only for us to prosper spiritually, but in other areas as well, so as to better serve Him. God desires that we be sound in mind and body, thriving in every way:

> Beloved, I pray that you may prosper in all things and be in health, just as your soul prospers (III John 2, NKJV).

We are to be whole so as to fulfill the believer's role in the kingdom of God—to manifest the heart of God (His character), the mind of God (His wisdom), and the hand of God (His power). In this, the man Christ Jesus is our example. We are to operate as the sons of God (more on this in Chapter 2).

The Bible teaches us that we are called to reign as kings and priests with Jesus in the kingdom of God (Revelation 1:6). As children of the kingdom, we are to start now by successfully exercising our authority in the spirit realm.

In order to grasp what is necessary to reign spiritually, let us look briefly at the story of David, following closely the path he traveled to gain the throne over the entire kingdom of Israel.

David's Path to Kingship

David did not simply inherit the throne and therefore reign over the nation of Israel. At first, David was but a shepherd boy; he was sent back to watch the sheep. His divine calling produced no immediate change in his living conditions. As of yet, there was little evidence of his anointing, and none of his calling to be king over Israel.

But he did learn important lessons as a shepherd, as he would through every stage of his maturation. As a shepherd, he learned to put the needs of his sheep before his own, and even risk his life for the sheep. (No wonder Jesus called Himself the Good Shepherd—He gave His life for His sheep.) David also learned humility, serving in what was considered the lowest class of people (after lepers).

The lesson that would serve David well his whole life—keeping his heart pure towards God even when he sinned—was simply, yet eloquently, spoken of by Paul: when we are weak, God can be strong in us:

> *And He said to me, "My grace is sufficient for you, for My strength is made perfect in weakness." Therefore most gladly I will rather boast in my infirmities, that the power of Christ may rest upon me. Therefore I take pleasure in infirmities, in reproaches, in needs, in persecutions, in distresses, for Christ's sake. For when I am weak, then I am strong* (2 Corinthians 12:9-10, NKJV).

It is not surprising, for one so gifted and dear to the Lord's own heart, that David's talents should be manifested from an early age. It did not take long for David to receive notice as a skillful musician. Not only that, he also became known as "a mighty valiant man, and a man of war, and prudent in matters, and a comely person, and the Lord... *was* with him" (I Samuel 16:18). Therefore it seemed fitting that David be appointed King Saul's personal musician. From that position, David gained favor with King Saul and was made his armor bearer. His calling and anointing began to be made apparent.

The next pivotal moment in David's life was his encounter with Goliath. In defeating Goliath, David helped win a great battle against the Philistines. By winning a great battle for the armies of Israel, David gained the favor of the nation. With the favor of the nation, David received the praise of the women. And with the praise of the women, David incurred the jealousy of Saul.

As a result, David began a period of his life in which he would live as a fugitive from the law, while still being a leader of Israel. It is interesting that, during this time of trial—while evading those who wanted to kill him—David began to learn how to rule over the nation. Not only did David learn to work effectively amid trying circumstances, David developed the ability to win over the opposition.

David exercised mercy, sparing Saul's life in the cave (I Samuel 24). He respected the Lord's anointed, repenting for the little wrong he had done in cutting off a corner of Saul's robe (v.4-6). And most of all, he repaid, or overcame, evil with good (Romans 12:17-21), causing Saul to exclaim, "You *are* more righteous than I" (I Samuel 24:17, NKJV). David kept his heart pure before God, seeking first His kingdom and His righteousness (Matthew 6:33); Saul could not help but see that light. Because of David's single-heartedness, God would give him all other things besides.

As a member of Saul's "cabinet," David behaved himself wisely, growing in wisdom. In fact, the Scriptures tell us that he "behaved himself more wisely than all the servants of Saul; so that his name was much set by" (I Samuel 18:30). He continued to fight battles on behalf of his people, always looking over his shoulder, lest Saul should find him and end his life.

He who should have most supported him, opposed him, and made it twice as difficult for him. David was doing good for Saul, routing the enemy, and yet Saul sought to take his life out of jealousy. How pure must our motives be in order to serve in the kingdom of God! How much we need God's own heart to do so!

In time, Saul was killed in a battle against the Philistines. The tribe of Judah, David's home tribe, promptly anointed him king over the house of Judah. So David began to reign from Hebron.

But the rest of Israel did not receive David's kingship so quickly. Abner, Saul's surviving chief of command, took Ishbosheth, one of Saul's sons, and anointed him to be king over the other eleven tribes of Israel.

Over the next few years, there was war between the followers of David and the followers of Saul (II Samuel 3:1). As time progressed,

David's followers began to gain the upper hand. Eventually, David won the whole nation over to his side. David exercised patience in coming into what God had for him, and balanced justice with mercy.

King David continued to reign because he reigned in the spirit first, watching his words, his actions, and the intentions of his heart. The fact that he still sinned reminded him of his need for God, and he genuinely repented. He knew his maturation in the spirit was a life-long process. As a child of the kingdom, David started by becoming built up in God, overcoming lesser difficulties initially, so as to surmount larger obstacles later.

Beginning the Reign

David's anointing by the prophet Samuel (I Samuel 16) began the fulfillment of the calling God had placed on David's life, which was to be king over all Israel, ruling from Jerusalem. But first he had to spend seven years and six months reigning over the tribe of Judah, from the city of Hebron. David's reign commenced at this point, but it was not complete: it was necessary that he start the exercise of his kingship over a smaller area than what was ultimately promised to him. As Christians, our learning to exercise dominion in the spiritual realm—the kingdom of God—is similar to David's experience of gaining kingship.

The New Testament has much to say about the kingdom of God. The four Gospels are filled with accounts of parables Jesus taught concerning the kingdom of God. Jesus went everywhere preaching "the Gospel of the kingdom of God" (Mark 1:14-15, Matthew 4:23-24, Luke 1:43). Jesus preached the good news of the kingdom—the authority and demonstrated power—of God. As children of the kingdom, we have been called to be the sons of God (John 1:12; I John 3:1). We have been called to reign as kings and priests unto God (Revelation 1:6, 5:10). We are also called to be imitators of God (Ephesians 5:1).

Just as David did, we have received our anointing. We have gained entrance into the kingdom of God. This we have done by being born of the water and of the Spirit (John 3:5). We are now making our calling and election sure:

> And we declare to you glad tidings—that promise which was made to the fathers. God has fulfilled this for us their children, in that He has raised up Jesus. As it is also written in the second Psalm: "You are my Son; today I have begotten

You." And that He raised Him from the dead, no more to return to corruption, He has spoken thus: "I will give you the sure mercies of David" [the holy and sure blessings promised to David] (Acts 13:32-34, NKJV).

We also understand that we cannot fully inherit all that is ours in this life. We understand that we will not receive our glorified bodies until after our death, or the rapture, whatever the case may be for us. But if, through faith and patience, we follow after the promises of God, the rewards will be everlasting:

Incline your ear and come to me. Hear, and your soul shall live. I will make an everlasting covenant with you—the sure mercies of David [God's faithful love promised to David] (Isaiah 55:3, NKJV).

God will remember His faithful ones. On that day, we will see Him! On that day, we will reign from the new Jerusalem! On that day, we will see the fulfillment of all that has been promised to us as the followers of God, and we will not be able to contain our amazement and joy.

In the meantime, we must undergo our "training." We are heirs, heirs of God, and joint-heirs with Christ (Romans 8:17). The heir, while he is a child, "is under tutors and governors until the time appointed of the father" (Galatians 4:1-2).

As David, we may spend time in learning to minister to others. As David, we may spend time being persecuted by others, some of whom are jealous of us. As David, we will spend time learning to rule over the kingdom. And as David, we will spend time exercising dominion over a part of the promises God has granted to us before we receive it in fulfillment.

As we undergo the new birth experience (Acts 2:38), and gain entrance into the kingdom of God (John 3:5), we begin a growth process in the spirit. We grow until we gain the maturity to exercise full dominion in this kingdom. We are preparing for a greater manifestation of the kingdom of God.

We must commence our reign in the spirit, gaining the throne over the tribe of Judah before ascending the throne of the nation of Israel. Learning to reign in Hebron, overcoming all obstacles and hindrances, we will in time reign from Jerusalem.

Only the Faithful Will Rule

He that will be faithful in reigning from Hebron will also be faithful in reigning from Jerusalem. He that is faithful over a small part of the kingdom will be faithful over the whole kingdom. Wherever we are, with whatever we are entrusted, it is imperative that we be faithful to do the will of God, in the exercise of His authority and power. God is looking for faithful servants.

In the parable of the three servants with the talents, Jesus said that the lord told the two good servants, "Thou hast been faithful over a few things, I will make thee ruler over many things" (Matthew 25:21,23; see also Luke 19:17,19).

Jesus also told us, "He that is faithful in that which is least is faithful also in much" (Luke 16:10). Indeed, we must be faithful in the exercise of the authority and power that we have now. Those who are faithful in the exercise of the kingdom of God in this life will be able to rule in the world that is to come. Only the faithful will reign. He that perseveres to the end will be saved:

> *And you will be hated by all for My name's sake. But he who endures to the end will be saved* (Matthew 10:22).

You have begun this race of faith already. Join me now in this journey of thought, as we travel down the path of ideas. Let us explore the power of the kingdom.

CHAPTER TWO
THE POWER OF A SON OF GOD

Ties to Supernatural Ability

Seeking to find power in the kingdom, by His Spirit, our glance naturally focuses on persons demonstrating supernatural abilities. The term "sons of God" calls attention to those exhibiting godlike qualities. For example, when Nebuchadnezzar, a heathen king, saw Shadrach, Meshach, and Abednego walking around in the fiery furnace with a fourth unknown man, he said that "the form of the fourth is like the Son of God" (Daniel 3:25).

Scholars have noted that this was not a statement understood in the confines of Christian terminology. They tell us this was not necessarily a statement of conversion. This was a pagan king, who saw an individual so far beyond the confines of the natural realm, that he could only describe Him as having godlike qualities. In other words, the fourth man in the fire must have had some connection with deity.

When the centurion witnessed the crucifixion of Jesus Christ, he also saw the startling signs which accompanied His suffering and death. He witnessed the darkness covering the land from noon until three in the afternoon. He beheld the earthquake that shook the area. He watched the rocks being torn and observed the graves being opened. He noted the resurrections that followed (Matthew 27:45-54; Mark 15:31-39).

When he regarded all that had happened, he said, "Truly this man was the Son of God." Again, scholars have remarked that this does not necessarily mean a conversion took place (although I would not doubt that it took place sooner or later). Nevertheless, the supernatural phenomena he experienced forged a strong connection in his mind, between this man hanging on the cross, and the supernatural or godlike qualities he must have possessed.

While Mark's Gospel focuses on the centurion alone, Matthew's account depicts several other witnesses reinforcing the centurion's testimony: When the centurion and those that were with him had witnessed the crucifixion of Jesus Christ, they made the statement, "Truly this was the Son of God" (Matthew 27:54). It has also been stated by scholars that this was not necessarily a statement of revelation as to Jesus' identity. Whether it is or not goes beyond the scope of this book.

Regardless of the position taken on spiritual revelation of the witnesses, their association of Jesus with the term, "Son of God," has a very powerful meaning: He was observed to command supernatural ability and power!

The phrase "Son of God" contains a strong allusion to the great powers of the supernatural world. They were saying that this was not just an ordinary man. He was not even merely an extraordinary man. This man, who had been crucified, was from the beyond. At the very least, they believed that this man had a close connection to deity.

Angels

The Old Testament refers to angels as the sons of God (Job 1:6; 2:1; 38:7; and, arguably, Genesis 6:1-4). They were called sons of God because they were like God in a sense. They were like God in that they have greater power, wisdom, and ability than other created beings. They demonstrate dominion over other parts of creation.

Theirs is a greater ability than man's. Man was made a little lower than the angels (Psalm 8:4-5). Angels are greater in power and might than the greatest of men, even the dignitaries among us (II Peter 2:11). They also possess greater wisdom than man does in his fallen state. When a certain lady was impressed with King David's wisdom, she paid him as high a compliment she could think of. She said, "My lord is wise, according to the wisdom of an angel of God" (II Samuel 14:20).

Angels have a specialty in strength; they excel in it (Psalm 103:20). They are supernatural, and so surpass the natural realm in their abilities. Thus, they have greater abilities than human beings possess.

They are the ones that carry out God's commands. When God moves in a supernatural way, He often acts through an angel. It is through angels that God carries out His laws in nature (Revelation 7:1). They also administer God's justice and mercy.

Angels carry out God's justice on earth. When the Lord destroyed Sodom and Gomorrah, He did it through angels (Genesis 19:12-22). It will also be through angels that the judgments are poured out in the Great Tribulation that is to come (Revelation 8-10).

The angels minister the Lord's mercy. When He shut the mouths of the lions in the den where Daniel was thrown, He did it through an angel (Daniel 6:22). He used an angel to bring the children of Israel out of the land of Egypt, and to lead them through the wilderness (Numbers 20:16; Exodus 23:20-23). An angel from heaven appeared to Jesus on the Mount of Olives, and strengthened him (Luke 22:43).

Angels were made a little higher than man, at least initially. They are, in a sense, godlike. Hence, they are referred to as "sons of God."

The Distinction Between God and All Others

Now, calling angels "sons of God" does not mean that angels are demigods or "little gods"; it is simply a descriptive term. We must remember that there is, and will always be, a distinction between the Creator and all of creation. That distinction must never be blurred. It is only to God Himself that we can pray, for only He can answer our prayers. We should never confuse an amazing creation with the deity of God, for He alone must be worshiped and adored.

To dare to cloud this distinction is to place yourself in danger of not only eternal judgment from God, but even possible judgment in this life. King Herod found this to be true when the angel of the Lord smote him so that he died (Acts 12:20-23). Herod tried to accept the praise of men calling him a god and he met with death. When you muddle the picture in this regard, you challenge the sovereignty of God. That is a dangerous position in which to be found.

The apostle Peter warned Cornelius about blurring this distinction (Acts 10:25-26). The apostles Barnabas and Paul understood that this line should not be crossed. They manifested this understanding when they refused to accept the worship of the people of Lystra by declaring that they were but men (Acts 14:11-18).

Even the apostle John was moved to worship an angel when he saw wondrous things. Instead of receiving the worship, the angel stopped him, saying that he was only a fellow servant. Then he told John to worship God (Revelation 19:10).

Contrast also the attitudes of two notable angels: Michael and Lucifer. Lucifer, one of the highest and most talented angels, was cast down from heaven because of his presumption (Isaiah 14:12-15). But Michael was willing to serve, and so was elevated.

His very name—Mi-cha-el in Hebrew—means, "who is like unto God." But, by his actions, Michael did not choose to interpret his name as one bringing glory upon himself. Instead, he turned it into a battle cry: "Who is like unto God?" His humility before God—and his tremendous love and respect for Him—were such that he would go to war with anyone who would have the audacity to proclaim himself, "like unto God."

This characteristic may be why God chose Michael to cast the dragon out of heaven, and down to the earth (Revelations 12:7-9). When the archangel was yet contending with the devil, disputing over the body of Moses, Jude 9 says that Michael "durst not bring against him a railing accusation, but said, 'The Lord rebuke thee.'" His words focused on God, not himself, and so invoked the Lord's power. Michael, unlike the devil, unswervingly respected God's sacred intention for the use of the tongue—to glorify Him alone—and so would not do otherwise. He refused to act as:

> ...these filthy dreamers [who] defile the flesh, despise dominion, and speak evil of dignities...But these speak evil of those things they know not: but what they know naturally, as brute beasts, in those things they corrupt themselves. Woe unto them! for they have gone the way of Cain, and ran greedily after the error of Balaam for reward, and perished in the gainsaying of Cor-e [Korah]... Raging waves of the sea, foaming out their own shame; wandering stars, to whom is reserved the blackness of darkness for ever (Jude 8,10-11,13).

Since pride was the sin that made the angels fall, the way of God's kingdom is humility and the obedient service of the tongue. Everyone who wants to be used of God denies himself (Matthew 16:24), so that God may be "all in all" (I Corinthians 15:28). They take the example of Jesus, who, even as God's Son, gave all that He had to give, "taking the form of a bondservant, and coming in the likeness of men" (Philippians 2:7, NKJV).

Only God is to be worshiped. The distinction between true deity and all the rest—which is simply creation—must never be lost. The Word of God and the name of Michael the archangel make this truth clear.

So the term, "sons of God," when used in relation to the angels, draws attention to the supernatural knowledge, wisdom, and power that the ministering spirits of God display. Their actions are supernatural; so is their being. As such, they surpass the abilities of man, going beyond that of the natural world. "Sons of God" refers to the godlike qualities of the angels, just as the term "sons of Belial" refers to the wicked qualities of Belial.

The Right to Travel the Road

The divinity of the Almighty is transcendent, wholly untouchable, reserved for God alone. Yet God has a plan for mankind, one in which He freely reveals a portion of His Divine nature with men, while losing nothing of Himself. In a real sense, God desires to make man like Himself—a privilege not given to any other created beings.

This relationship speaks of an intimate collaboration between God and men. God chose to reveal to mankind His divine nature. God even became man, so that man could become like God. Jesus assumed our human nature so that we could take on His own.

The angels are called the "sons of God," but they are not the only ones to receive that distinction. John 1:12-13 tells us of those people who will be given a unique right: to become the sons of God in a new and living way—by receiving Jesus Christ, believing in His Name, and being born of God.

As His people, we have been given the right to undergo the process to become the sons of God, but we acknowledge that it will be a process—God's thoughts and ways are so far above our own. The apostle John stated that, although we are called the sons of God now, the full working out of it has not yet been achieved (I John 3:1-2), but will be completed when Jesus comes again.

Still, we have been given the right to undergo the process of becoming the sons of God. Paul clarifies this by stating that when we are led by the Spirit of God, we demonstrate that we are the sons of God (Romans 8:14).[1] In order to be led by the Spirit, and come into our inheritance as sons, Paul warned that we need to watch our words, so that we may be blameless, without fault, as the sons of God:

Do all things without murmurings and disputings: That ye may be blameless and harmless, the sons of God, without rebuke (Philippians 2:14-15).

So the term "sons of God" links us in close connection to His deity—being like God Himself—especially when we keep ourselves pure in thought, word, and action:

...but we know that when He is revealed, we shall be like Him, for we shall see him as He is. And everyone who has this hope in Him purifies Himself, just as He is pure (I John 3:2-3, NKJV).

Called to Be Like God

The Bible describes the Lord as "the God of gods" (Daniel 11:36). Jesus quoted the Scripture when He said, "Ye are gods" (John 10:34; Psalm 82:6), thus naming us as the gods, of whom He is Lord. How can we be called "gods?" Reading the second half of Psalm 82:6, we see that our being called "gods" is linked to being named "children of the Most High." We are godlike creations, made in the image of God and in His likeness (Genesis 1:26-27;5:1-2).

Of course, the statement, "Ye are gods," is not to be taken in the sense that New Agers believe—that we are all gods, and are thus our own source of morality, law, and existence. This type of thinking is pure heresy; it exalts itself against the knowledge of God. Remember always to keep the distinction between the Creator and creation visible.

Yet, there is that sense where we are called to be like God. This is why we find a number of biblical commands exhorting us to be holy because the Lord is holy (I Peter 1:16) or to pattern ourselves after the Lord (I Peter 2:21;4:1). Paul told us to be "imitators of God" (Ephesians 5:1).[2] Jesus even informed us that we were to be perfect, as our Father in heaven is perfect (Matthew 5:48).

So we are to grow in our "sonship." This is the will of God for those who follow Him. Presently, we are only the sons of God in part. But as our eyes stay on Him, we are changed into the same image. Paul wrote:

> But we all, with open face beholding as in a glass the glory of the Lord, are changed into the same image from glory to glory, even as by the Spirit of the Lord (II Corinthians 3:18).

> Now we see through a glass darkly; but then face to face: now I know in part; but then shall I know even as also I am known (I Corinthians 13:12).

Paul was certain to let us know that creation is longingly looking forward to the day when there will be the full manifestation of the sons of God (Romans 8:19). This is their earnest expectation. This is their desperate yearning and aspiration. All creation is waiting for us to fully become the sons of God. All creation is waiting for us to become what we were designed to be.

The Fullness of God

In Ephesians 3:14-19, Paul talks about a prayer he prayed concerning the Church. One of the significant hopes he expresses for the

Church is that we would "be strengthened with might by His Spirit in the inner man" (v.16). Our inner man—our spirit—must be made strong for His purpose.

Paul then closes his prayer for God's will to be done in us, saying that he would like us to be strengthened so as to "be filled with all the fullness of God" (v.19). Does he really mean that we all could be filled with **all** the **fullness** of **God**? If we were still in doubt, Paul goes on to make the now famous statement, God "is able to do exceeding abundantly above all that we ask or think, **according to the power that worketh in us**" (v.20).

We will be filled with the fullness of God, in His time. But we must first be strengthened with might, by His Spirit, in the inner man. We must be so fortified in every degree in order to be filled with, and contain, all the fullness of God. Therefore, we must be empowered with God's demonstrated abilities—*dunamis* in Greek—in our inner man. (Later, in Chapters 3, 6, 12, and 14, we will cover the role that words play in helping us to be strengthened with might in the inner man.)

Paul prayed that we would "be able to comprehend with all saints what is the breadth, and length, and depth, and height" (v.18). And just in case we fail to understand the extent of this, Paul told us that God is able to do far beyond all the things that we could ask or imagine. Then to sum it up, he said that God was able to do all these great things **according to the power that works in us** (v.20).

If we only allow the power of God to work in us to a small degree, then we will only see God do little things. If we allow the power of God to work in us freely, then the door will be open for God to do things that far surpass our imagination. It is all based on the extent to which we are willing to allow the power of God to work in us.

Again, we have been granted the right to be called the sons of God. We have the form of godliness; let us not deny the power thereof. Paul said, "For as many as are led by the Spirit of God, they are the sons of God" (Romans 8:14). It all starts with being led by the Spirit of God. The way to be sensitive to the Spirit is to be obedient to what God says, and to respond in faith to what God is doing. The apostle Peter wrote:

According as his divine power hath given unto us all things that pertain unto life and godliness [i.e., his divine power has granted us everything that is connected to true life and to **the likeness of God**], *through the knowledge of him that hath* *called us to glory and virtue: Whereby are given unto us exceeding great and precious promises:* that by these ye might be **partakers of the divine nature,** *having escaped the corruption that is in the world through lust* (II Peter 1:3-4, emphasis added).

Peter told us that we have been given all things that pertain to life and godliness. To accompany this, we have been granted exceeding great and precious promises. By these promises, we are to become partakers of the divine nature. We have access to His nature. We can partake of it. And His promises are given to us to facilitate our becoming more like Him. Peter went on to say that we should be even more diligent to make our call and election sure..."so an entrance shall be ministered unto you abundantly into the everlasting kingdom of our Lord and Saviour Jesus Christ" (II Peter 1:11).

Through this whole process, we will be granted an entrance into the kingdom that Jesus talked about. We will gain access to the kingdom that Jesus obviously claimed as His own (Luke 23:42). We will have an entrance into the kingdom of God ministered to us **abundantly.** Then, truly, the kingdom will come for us as we have been taught to pray (Matthew 6:10; Luke 11:2).

Jesus, our chief example in being a Son of God, shows us how to bring about the kingdom. According to Luke 4:1, Jesus was first of all full of the Holy Ghost. Second, He was led by the Spirit (into the desert). As a result, Luke 4:14 tells us that He returned in the power of the Spirit. Jesus, the Son of God, then healed the sick, gave sight to the blind, opened deaf ears, caused the dumb to speak, made the leper whole, raised the dead, and cast out devils.

We, as His disciples, are to go and do likewise. In Matthew 10:8, He told His followers,

Heal the sick, cleanse the lepers, raise the dead, cast out devils: freely ye have received, freely give.

He told them that they were to accomplish these works. The sons of God are called to perform these demonstrations of power and bring about the kingdom on earth.

The promise to partake of His nature is scriptural. We are called to be the sons of God. We are to grow in the spirit until we have been filled with all the fullness of God, and then release His power to the world. All of creation is waiting for us to do so (Romans 8:19).

---

[1]David Sanzo, *Power to Tread on Serpents* (Roanoke, VA: Spirit of Life, 1992), 66-68.
[2]Ibid., 74-75

CHAPTER THREE
THE POWER OF GODLINESS

The Form of Godliness

Christians, who want the fullness of what God has for us, need to live with hearts totally devoted to God, acting in the power of the Spirit. We need true godliness—to be inspired and directed by the truth, the Word of God—which will cause our calling as sons of God to be manifested in power.

But there are pitfalls to be wary of. To have God's power guided by imperfect or incomplete godliness may very well lead to ruin—that is why we need the fullness of God. To whom much is given, much is expected (Luke 12:48). And to have a form of godliness, but deny its power, is equally, if not more disastrous. We need to be careful not to lead astray any of our Lord's beloved (Luke 17:1-2).

Paul warned us that in the last days people would arise who are described as "having a form of godliness, but denying the power thereof" (II Timothy 3:5). According to Paul, we need to turn away from these individuals, for they have (or have been affected by) a form of godliness only, without substance.

The Greek word behind "form" is *morphosin,* which means "having the appearance or the external form." *Eusebeias* is the word behind godliness (God-likeness), which is concerned with instilling a reverential feeling, piety, devotion, or religion.

We are warned concerning those that have the appearance of being a Christian. On the surface, they look godly. They seem to be pious and devoted to God. To view them with the natural eye, you would be convinced they are truly followers or disciples of Jesus Christ. They are affected by godliness, but lack a vital ingredient, which is reason for alarm.

The Greek root word behind "power" is *dunamis.* This word refers not only to ability or potential but to actual working power, energy on display, the dynamics of things. It is the actual work being accomplished. You can see its fruit or results being acted out; you see the work being performed. It is not just the capability but the exhibition of power.

We need godliness filled with, and displaying, God's power. If we want God, but do not want His fullness, we deny Him altogether. For if we are not for Him with all of our being, we are against Him:

> *He that is not with me is against me: and he that gathereth not with me scattereth* (Luke 11:23).

It is not enough to be with the Master; you must do what He does, with Him at your side, with your heart in His. Your life must be hidden with Christ in God (Colossians 3:3). The example of the seven sons of Sceva (Acts 19:13-16) is sufficient warning for the branches not to detach themselves from the vine, for without Him we can do nothing (see John 15:5-8). We need to avoid being like Saul, who sought his own glory, and become like David, seeking God's work and timing, to obtain the fullness of God.

Denying the Power

The word behind "denying" is *ernemenoi,* which means to deny, disclaim, renounce, decline, refuse, and even contradict. Some people can deny—disclaim, renounce, and even refuse—the actual working of the power of godliness in their lives. If that were not enough, they even take steps to contradict the teachings and the power of godliness in their lives. How is this done? How do people deny the working of God in their lives? How do they deny the power of godliness or God-likeness? There are several ways.

First of all, it would be easy to point out those that have bought into the New Age type of thinking. They desire to be like a god. They want to have godlike qualities. Many of them are devout to their "religion." They will consistently set aside time for prayer or "meditation." They place much confidence in crystals, symbols, superstition, or various other forms of witchcraft.

However, they deny the power of Jesus Christ, which supersedes all. They believe He is only one of many good teachers who have gone before, instead of "the Christ, the Son of the living God" (Matthew 16:16). So they diminish His person, His identity, and who He really is.

The result is that they may exercise some power from another world, but they deny the working power of the one true God. They have a form of godliness, but they deny the existence of the one supreme God of the universe, and His close interactions with men.

"The Anti-supernaturalists"

Another category of people who have the appearance of godliness, but deny the power thereof, is what I call "the anti-supernaturalists." This group can be divided into two camps. The first is comprised of those who disbelieve the occurrence of supernatural works accomplished by God, as described in the Scriptures. These are easily dismissed as not truly being Christian, for they do not even believe the Scriptures on which Christianity is founded.

The other camp is made up of those who "believe" in Jesus Christ and seem to adhere to the Scriptures. The problem is that they either deny the supernatural ability of God to work *today* in a believer's life to heal, deliver, and change individuals, or else they deny His willingness to do so.

They claim that miracles, tongues, and the operation of the gifts of the Spirit are not for today. They try to limit the operation of God to a specific period of time or to a group of individuals. And they deny God's ability or willingness to heal someone today or to otherwise work supernaturally. They disclaim the willingness of God to deliver someone at once from bondages such as drugs, alcohol, or other things. They discount the work of angels among us. Or they refuse to acknowledge as real some of the other supernatural aspects of God, which are so clearly described in the Scriptures.

"Christians" Who Deny the Power

Yet another way to be affected by the form of godliness, but refuse its working power, involves Christians who can be classified in one of the two categories that follow. The first category deals with those that have a form of worship, a form of prayer, but only an appearance of Christianity. Their problem is that they refuse to allow prayer and worship to change their lives, to change them as persons. They insist on living in sin; they will not allow the Holy Spirit to change their hearts or affect their lifestyles.

Sure, they seem to have the contours of Christianity, but they disallow the workings of godliness to have any effect on them. They dismiss any restriction on their lusts as being "legalistic." They claim only to follow the "grace" of God without allowing it to change them. It would seem that they have been affected by "the man of sin," "the son of perdition" (see II Thessalonians 2:3-13).

Now, I am not talking about following man-made laws, which are fallible. The leading of the Spirit of God, however, is not. Neither is His Word fallible. Yet these, the Spirit and the Word, are what some Christians circumvent. The apostle Paul, who is sometimes referred to as the "revelator of grace," wrote to Titus about this denial in practice. He said,

> They *profess that they know God; but* **in works they deny him**, *being abominable, and disobedient, and unto every good work reprobate* (Titus 1:16, emphasis added).

He went on in the first ten verses of the next chapter to describe what sound doctrine was. He began to teach how not to deny God in works. Then he said,

> *For* **the grace of God** *that bringeth salvation* **hath appeared** *to all men,* **teaching us that, denying ungodliness and worldly lusts, we should live soberly, righteously, and godly,** *in this present world* (Titus 2:11-12, emphasis added).

Other "Christians" Who Deny the Power

Christians who deny the power in the first sense, due to lawlessness, do not allow the Spirit of God to have any control over their finances, their conduct, their appearance, or the direction of their lives. They fail to see that God is interested in every part of their lives and every part of their being. Thus, they retain a form of godliness, but deny its power, and so frustrate the grace of God. They deny, and miss out on, what God would like to do in their lives.

The other side of this coin contains those who do live by a standard of conduct, but their hearts are unchanged, resulting in legalism. They have been taught to live by certain rules that may be right or pleasing to God, but their attitudes are not Christlike. Therefore, they become critical and judgmental of those that are not just like them.

On the outside, they seem to have mastered everything religiously, but on the inside they are "full of dead men's bones" (Matthew 23:27); they have no life inside them. The gentle peace of God is not ruling their heart and life.

They have their appearance of godliness, but they deny its working power in themselves, in their inner man. They live only by the letter and neglect the flow of life from the Spirit of God. Therefore, they die spiritually, "for the letter killeth, but the Spirit giveth life" (II Corinthians 3:6).

The Free-flow of Liberty

Where the flow of the Spirit of the Lord is, there is liberty (II Corinthians 3:17). Liberty does not proceed from an automaton or robot. Freely choosing to abide by the spirit of the law, we are not controlled, frozen, as it were, into a rigid, compulsory existence.

However, we are not to live simply as we please: we are to live rightly, not out of mere obligation, but out of our sincere willingness to do so. We are not to use our liberty for the fulfillment of carnal desires (Galatians 5:13), so we willingly submit to the control (illumination, leadership, protection, and guidance) of the Spirit of Life. Therefore we do not live as the flesh pleases, but as the Spirit of God pleases (Romans 6:16). The Spirit brings balance, helping us avoid extremes, excesses, and abuses. The free-flow of liberty is brought about by the action of the Spirit, which keeps us in right relation to the truth.

In order to keep our liberty in the Spirit, Paul told us that we were to turn away from those that deny the power of godliness. The Greek word behind the term "turn away" is *apotrethoo,* which can also be translated "to avoid or shun." Paul was pretty serious about turning away from those that renounced the working power of God.

Of course, this does not mean that we are to be hateful to them. Christian love ought to be evident in all that we say and do; nevertheless, we are to avoid and even shun this type of thing ("love the sinner, hate the sin"). Furthermore, we are to turn away from those who embrace this pattern of life, so that they may realize their need of repentance.

Remember, the apostle James said that we were not to be hearers only of the Word, but also doers. If we are hearers only, then we deceive ourselves. We may have that appearance of godliness but we are denying its essential working power.

Since our words are extensions of our spirit (more on this topic in Chapter 5), we can say that we are to be "doers of the Spirit"—obedient to the voice of the Spirit speaking personally to us, as well as to the written Word. When the Spirit of God speaks to us concerning a matter, we need to obey.

CHAPTER FOUR
THE BEGINNINGS OF FAITH

Starting the Race of Faith

In order to be doers of the Word, obedient to the Spirit, we can learn much from Hebrews 11. Often called the "faith chapter" of the Bible, Hebrews 11 relates the acts of some of the heroes of faith. Among these heroes were those who offered a more excellent sacrifice to God (v.4). One was taken up into heaven, so as not to see death. Another built an ark to save their posterity. Others left their homeland to look for a city whose builder and maker is God. There were those who were delivered from Egypt, being led out by the mighty hand of God. They passed through the Red Sea on dry ground. Others saw the walls of Jericho fall flat. It also refers to other outstanding witnesses:

> *Who through faith subdued kingdoms, wrought righteousness, obtained promises, stopped the mouths of lions, Quenched the violence of fire, escaped the edge of the sword, out of weakness were made strong, waxed valiant in fight, turned to flight the armies of the aliens. Women received their dead raised to life again: and others were tortured, not accepting deliverance; that they might obtain a better resurrection: And others had trial of cruel mockings and scourgings, yea, moreover of bonds and imprisonment: They were stoned, they were sawn asunder, were tempted, were slain with the sword; they wandered about in sheepskins and goatskins; being destitute, afflicted, tormented; (Of whom the world was not worthy:) they wandered in deserts, and in mountains, and in dens and caves of the earth* (Hebrews 11:33-38).

These people are our models of faith. From this chapter we see that faith is related to our salvation, and is essential in order to please God. Faith is vital to our well-being and to obtaining promises from God based on His Word. It is the key to our overcoming the world, and to our future resurrection.

The writer of Hebrews went on to say that in spite of the great things that were accomplished by them through faith, these heroes of faith would "not be made perfect" without us (v.40). Without us, they could not be made complete. Yet, they did show to us *the beginnings of faith,* the first stages of faith.

With all of this in mind, the writer opens the next chapter by admonishing us to:

> *Lay aside every weight, and the sin which doth so easily beset us, and let us run with patience the race that is set before us, Looking unto Jesus the author and finisher of our faith* (Hebrews 12:1-2a).

The context of this passage clearly shows that the race set before us has to do with the exercise of our faith. It is a race of faith. Paul even said that it was a fight of faith (I Timothy 6:12). We understand faith very simply to be believing in God, and this is indeed the foundation of faith. However, there is a difference between our western view and the Hebrew perception of believing in God.

In the Jewish mind-set, faith or believing in God does not stop with simply agreeing with the idea of the existence of God; it includes the action that accompanies the belief. This does not mean that we are saved by works. Nor does it mean that we can accomplish spiritual things through fleshly works. But works must accompany faith or that faith cannot be said to be valid or effective. We read in James 2, that "faith, if it hath not works, is dead, being alone" (v.17), and, "faith without works is dead" (v.26).

The Hebrew language, being a pictorial language, is based on what you can see. If you can see it, you can say it. Therefore, faith must have evidence in order to say it exists. For it to be faith, it must be more than mental acquiescence: there must be a substance to faith (Hebrews 11:1), which involves evidence.

In simple terms, faith is believing in God. But this foundational concept of simply trusting in God just gets us started in the "race of faith"; it is only the beginning, whereas there is a whole race to run. It is not he who starts well, but he who finishes well, that will receive the prize:

> *He that endureth* **to the end** *shall be saved* (Matthew 10:22, emphasis added).

Sometimes, though, there are things that trip us up, or weigh us down, while we attempt to run this race of faith. If we would courageously fight this fight of faith, we would learn to lay aside the weights that interfere with our exercise of faith. Then this fight will become a race, and we will finish it well.

Words Contain Power

There is a cliché, often taught to youngsters, to help them not to lose control of themselves when someone begins to call them derogatory names. The children are taught to say, "Sticks and stones may break my bones, but words will never hurt me."

Yet, the longer we live, the more we understand that, in reality, this is simply not true. We know that if a parent continually tells a child he or she is no good, the child will soon behave accordingly. If a teacher continually tells a student that he or she is stupid, sooner or later the student is apt to become discouraged at learning. They will come to believe that they truly are intellectually inferior. On the other hand, if a sales manager continually tells his employees that they are able to reach a particular goal in the sale of a product or service, they will often accomplish just that.

Words are powerful, often carrying more than one meaning in themselves. Words can also have a range of effects, depending on the speaker's inflection or tone of voice, and the listener's interpretation. The same words spoken by two different people can mean different things. Words coming from one person can be received differently by others, depending on their cultural backgrounds, education, life experiences, etc. The same words coming from the same person may even be interpreted differently by the same hearer.

Words carry multiple interpretations, based on any number of factors. We must understand that much can be attributed to the speaker's attitude at the moment. For example, believers must be wary of what they speak, especially when they are hungry, angry, lonely, tired ("H.A.L.T."). Unchecked, negative emotions will darken the words you speak, just as positive emotions—fulfillment, love, a sense of belonging, and contentment—will lighten your speech, and buoy up your hearer(s).

Meaning is often hinged on the one word in the statement that you want to emphasize. Most of us have heard that a single statement of ten words can convey ten different meanings, depending on which of the ten words the emphasis is placed. Even a single word contains power.

We have also been told of the power of suggestion. The "positive mental attitude" people have told us that when we simply affirm a desire vocally, it will aid us in seeing that desire brought to pass. So the overweight are told that they should tell themselves every day, "I am going to lose these fifty pounds." Smokers remind themselves, "I am going to kick this smoking habit." Athletes tell themselves that they are going to break their own records. The salesman tells himself that he will close the deal.

Some tell us that we should look in the mirror every day and say, "Each day, and in every way, I am getting better, and better, and better." Proponents of "positive mental attitude" keep encouraging this type of behavior because they have discovered that there is a tremendous power in speaking a thing out first. Things tend to happen when you speak it out of your mouth. This is because words truly are powerful. Once you speak it long enough, you tend to believe it. Words release power. You may fulfill your own prophesy in action, without even being conscious of the fact. If you say, "I'm going to fail," chances are you will, because you have already given up. If however, you say something like, "I can do all things in Christ who strengthens me" (Philippians 4:13, NKJV), you most likely will. So speak "faith words."

Tying Your Shoes

As a child growing up, sibling rivalry was strong between my older brother and me. Anything that he was able to do, I expected to do as well. In fact, the competitive edge was so strong in me that I expected myself to be able to do all that my cousin was able to do, even though he was more than four years older than I was.

I remember being three years of age when my older brother learned to tie his shoes. He was five years old at the time. My cousin already knew how to tie his shoes. So it stood to reason in my mind that I should be able to do the same.

But no matter how hard I tried, my three-year-old mind could not grasp the concept. It was either that, or my fingers were not coordinated well enough to accomplish the feat. Whatever the case was, it was beyond my abilities at the time. So, naturally, I grew very frustrated.

To appease me, my mother and father told me that I would learn how to tie my shoes when I was five. They also told me that I would be allowed to go to school when I turned five. My parents also told me that I would be promoted to the Sunday class that I wanted to attend when I turned five. That was the class with all the "cool" kids. It seems all of life would have to wait until I was five years old. I wondered if I could ever catch up, after getting such a late start.

I would periodically attempt to tie my shoelaces and, as always, I was met with defeat. Eventually, I figured that I would have to wait until I was five before I would know how to tie my shoes. I guessed that the capability for it would magically appear once I was five years old. So I resigned myself to that fact. After all, "Mom and Dad do know what they are talking about, don't they?"

For a long time (at least several months it seems) I did not even try to tie my shoes. Then on the day I turned five, I dressed myself, except for putting on my sneakers. Then I grabbed them along with my little stool (my father had made one for each of us three sons at the time) and went to the kitchen. My mother was there at the time, so I knew that she could tie my laces for me. Then, of course, I could face the day with my agenda, and accomplish all the great feats that my young mind had conjured up.

When I entered the kitchen, my mother was temporarily busy. So I had to wait until she was free to tie my shoes. Then, without even thinking about it, I put my sneakers on and began to tie the laces. I was not even concentrating on what I was doing. But when I was finished and realized what I had done, I exploded with excitement—I could hardly believe it—I had tied my shoes!

Then I remembered that it was my birthday. Today I turned five years old. Talk about exhilaration! My parents actually did know what they were talking about. Knowing how to tie your shoes *did* magically appear once you turned five. It really did come with the territory.

Imagine my excitement: I was absolutely thrilled at my accomplishment. I do not remember what my mother's reaction was (probably "Oh, that's a good boy") but I could hardly believe it. I was in pure ecstasy!

With this experience behind me, I am sure you can see how confident I became concerning all the things that my parents told me. It stood to reason that their other predictions would also come to pass. You see, my parents knew what they were talking about. Now my life could begin.

Of course, you can guess how perplexed I became when they told me I still had to wait until September before I could enter kinder-garten. That was a whole two and a half months away—quite near a lifetime! I was sure that by then I would be far behind all the other students who began attending school on the day they turned five. Besides, I did not like the idea of being behind—I wanted to be ahead. Nevertheless, I did have to wait.

Now, obviously I did not tell this chapter of my life just to help somebody wanting to learn to tie their shoelaces (though I wonder how many parents may try it now with their children). The point is that my parents had spoken a word. I believed that word. And that word came to pass in my life.

Though they did not realize it themselves, they had released a word of faith into my life that was strong enough to come to pass. Even though I was not aware of the date, and was not consciously working towards its fulfillment, it still happened in perfect timing. My spirit grabbed a hold of their word and worked to bring it to pass.

Could all this be coincidence? I suppose anything can be marked off as being coincidental. You could say that it is a coincidence that every time I flip the switch, the light brightens the room. However, the more I live my life, the more convinced I become that it has less to do with coincidence, and a whole lot more to do with God and the laws that He has set in motion.

He has set physical laws in motion to govern the physical world. He has set biological laws in motion to govern the biological world. He likewise has set spiritual laws in motion to govern the spiritual world. Those spiritual laws govern the operation of faith and all of its results.

How do the spiritual laws work concerning words? In the next chapter, we will examine the spirit of a word.

CHAPTER FIVE
THE SPIRIT OF A WORD
The "Train" Behind a Word

There are definite spiritual laws concerning words. The following contains loose-fitting terminology, but it may help you to understand how powerful a word can be. It should also aid you in knowing how to discern the spiritual origins of words.

First of all, as immaterial constructions, "thoughts" properly reside in, or belong to, the spirit world. Thoughts relate to ideas, concepts, temptations, lusts, worship, etc. When we talk about thoughts that relate to these subjects, we could almost identify them with the spirits which attach to, and become the spirits of, these concepts.

The way a spirit will normally manifest itself to you is in the form of a thought. The body of the spirit is in the thought, so to speak. If a lustful spirit gets a hold of someone, that person will be thinking lustful thoughts. **When you entertain a thought, you entertain that spirit.** This should call our attention to what types of thoughts are prevailing in our minds, and who is behind them.

A word, whether spoken or written, is a representation of a thought. When the word "giraffe" is brought to our attention, we immediately picture a long-necked beast. This is because we have learned that the word "giraffe" is a representation of that particular animal. Likewise the word "rhinoceros" will bring to mind a sizable and powerful animal, with a single horn coming out of the middle of his face.

Therefore, if a word is a representation of a thought and that thought is the body of a spirit, we can see how *the word is an extension of the spirit.* When a word is spoken, it shows us the spirit to which it belongs.

The Scriptures tell us that "out of the abundance of the heart the mouth speaketh" (Matthew 12:34). The term "heart" in the Bible is often used to refer to what we sometimes call the subconscious mind or the spirit world. Here, Jesus is teaching us that the words spoken by our mouths come from the abundance, or the overflow of the spirit, under whose influence we are.

For example, when we receive the Holy Ghost, something happens with the words we are speaking. As one preacher said, "You cannot be filled with the Spirit without speaking."³ A new spirit has been placed within us.

The Spirit of God fills you, which is why we often use the term, "filled with the Holy Ghost." This new spirit needs an outlet, and uses the tongue, because words are an extension of the spirit. That is why you speak with tongues when you receive the gift of the Holy Ghost: He fills you and then extends or manifests Himself by speaking words that originate from Him, rather than you, the human vessel He now indwells.

Your Words Reveal Your Spirit

Now if a word is an extension of our spirit, then what do our words say about us? What do they say about our spirit: is it indicative of the Holy Spirit that dwells in us—or is it indicative of some other type of spirit prevalent in our lives?

If we speak vulgarity and other corrupt communication, we are not being ruled by the Holy Spirit of God. If we involve ourselves in slander and gossiping, we are not under the influence of the Holy Ghost. If we are backbiting, we are not abiding in the tabernacle of the Lord (Psalm 15:3).

If we bite and devour one another, we will be consumed one of another (Galatians 5:15). This is not the result of God's Spirit at work; this is an ungodly spirit manifesting itself. "Death and life *are* in the power of the tongue" (Proverbs 18:21). The spirit behind death, and the spirit behind life, are both made evident through the words of our mouth.

As a young preacher in Bible college, I noticed that the people who had power with God were the ones who did not yield their tongues to criticism. They were not involved in gossiping. They were not interested in character assassinations.

On the other hand, I would find pockets of people who thought they were spiritual, or desired some spiritual things, but they never did control their tongue. (Unfortunately, I still find these pockets of people on occasion.) They always found a reason to run somebody down. They enjoyed pointing out the weaknesses of others to make themselves look good. You could always count on them to point out the faults of all other parties. Great fault-finders they were, as long as they were not looking for their own.

Unkind words do not originate from the Holy Spirit. As a result, I did not feel comfortable hanging around these individuals. Clearly,

God was not very comfortable either. There was no consistency in the moving of the Spirit of God through their lives. When it happened, it was sporadic. Often, it was weak and anemic. Often, it was mishandled. This, in turn, would lead to unprofitable ends and obtain counter-productive results. "No man can serve two masters" (Matthew 6:24), or "be partakers of the Lord's table, and the table of devils" (I Corinthians 10:21).

The Spirit of Vengeance

In Luke 9:51-56, Luke records the story of Jesus and His followers traveling on their way to Jerusalem. On their way, they had to pass by a village occupied by the Samaritans. Although messengers were sent before them to make preparations for Him, the Samaritans would not receive Jesus because of His intentions to go to Jerusalem. They had some serious racial problems.

When James and John saw this, they became upset. They wanted to call fire down out of heaven to consume them as Elijah had done. But when they asked for Jesus' permission to do so, Jesus firmly rebuked them saying, "Ye know not what manner of spirit ye are of."

They had cause to be upset with the Samaritans' racist attitudes. But the apostles were not aware of the spirit that was motivating them, which stood behind their words. Although they did not realize it, their words showed what spirit was prompting them. The spirit that was prodding them was not in line with the will of God. Therefore, Jesus rebuked them for having the wrong spirit.

We must be careful that our words do not reveal a vengeful spirit. This is not a matter of simply concealing a wrong spirit—we need to have a right spirit within us.

Jesus once directed his followers not to worry about what they were to say when taken before the authorities. He said, "For it is not ye that speak, but the Spirit of your Father which speaketh in you" (Matthew 10:20).

If they contemplated beforehand what they were going to say, then their words would have their origin in their own human spirit. Their effect would be minimal, if not counter-productive. However, if they would just allow the Spirit of God to take control, the right words—the wisdom of God—would come out of their mouths.

Peter wrote that Christ left us an example, that we should follow his steps (I Peter 2:21). In the next two verses, Peter focuses on

31

Jesus's peaceful and peace-making disposition, especially during try-ing circumstances:

> Who did no sin, neither was guile found in his mouth: Who when he was reviled, reviled not again; when he suffered, he threatened not....

If we would follow Jesus' example, we will inherit blessings:

> Not rendering evil for evil, or railing for railing: but contrari-wise blessing; knowing that ye are thereunto called, that ye should inherit a blessing (I Peter 3:9).

Evidence of a Corrupted Spirit

The Bible lays out certain evidences or actions that we are to show (or not show) in order to bring our actions in line with the Spirit of God. For example, those that do the works of the flesh—manifesting products or results in a course of action initiated by the flesh—will not inherit the kingdom of God (Galatians 5:19-21).

Some of these mentioned works of the flesh are well understood. These include adultery, fornication, hatred (having to do with discord, feuds, and alienation), heresies (false doctrines, philosophies, etc.), envyings, murders, and drunkenness.

Others are not so widely understood. Uncleanness refers to lewd-ness or impurity of motives. Lewdness is described as "showing, or intended to excite, lust or sexual desire, specially in an offensive way."[4] This is where sexual harassment is played out: those that sexu-ally harass others are often lewd in their actions and words.

Lewdness is not only shown by conduct but is also born out by the way some people dress. They allow their flesh to dictate their tastes and values to them. One of the ways that it shows is in their appearance. Their motives are impure; they desire to incite lust. Their motives are not indicative of the pure Spirit of God at work.

In addition, lewdness is described as being "unlearned, ignorant, unprincipled, vicious."[5] Our words should not be unclean, or lewd.

Shocking the World

Lasciviousness refers to a lack of self-control, insolence (being rude, overbearing, and disrespectful), and outrageous behavior. It has to do with being undisciplined and unmanageable. It can also refer to being sexually loose or unrestrained.

It seems our modern society thrives on the "shock-value" of personalities, television talk shows, and other productions. We tend to champion those who are not restrained in their immorality. The more unrestricted they are (whether in appearance or conduct), the more they are celebrated.

This lasciviousness is a work of the flesh. As such, if it is found in our lives, it interferes with our inheriting the kingdom of God.

Webster also describes lasciviousness as "being characterized by or expressing lust and a tendency to excite lustful desires." This clearly is demonstrated through pornography and many modern movies, TV shows, and commercials. It seems that sex is used to sell every product on the market. This is a work of the flesh. It is an appeal to the flesh.

Also appealing to the flesh is the idea of reveling. Reveling contains the idea of lascivious feasting. It has to do with the "party" spirit (as in the "carousing" type of parties) and includes the idea of rioting. It is the participation in wild, uncontrollable partying. Unfortunately, some people look to their weekends just for this opportunity.

Just to clarify, this is surely not to say that Christians ought not to have fun. Nor do I mean that we cannot demonstrate exuberance in having a good time. What is alarming is a total lack of self-control, giving the flesh the opportunity to fulfill its lusts. This lawlessless leads to sin and death. And with our words, iniquity begins to take effect.

Since the Bible describes our tongue as the rudder of our ship (James 3:4-5), we must first guard our words from leading us in the direction of sin. Much of the cursing that goes on today could be simply classified as lascivious speech. Our conversations ought not to be that of uncontrolled speech—rude, overbearing, or disrespectful—which leads to uncontrolled action.

Neither should our words be intended to excite lust in others, for to consider the body as a means for pleasure alone is a form of idolatry. We understand idolatry to be the worship of an image, or the god represented by it. It may also be defined as placing anything, or pleasure, in God's place. We must not worship the body. For God to be God in your life, He must have no rivals.

In addition to promoting mankind's increasing addiction to sex, our words have also aided the rapid rise in psychics, New Age gurus, and others, by consulting those dealers in witchcraft, or the occult. The Greek word behind witchcraft is *pharmakeia,* which denotes not only "sorcery, magic, and enchantment," but also the employment of mind-altering drugs.

In our western world, it seems that there is no shortage of these consciousness-changing substances, whether it be cocaine, heroine, or some other "pharmaceutical" drug used to control depression, rages, hyperactivity, and so forth. This practice is spiritually dangerous. What is even more startling is that younger and younger children are taking these drugs, and in greater quantities, mixing different kinds of drugs, resulting in deadly effects. We are not to partake of any of the works of the flesh, including witchcraft in any of its forms.

Destruction begins with the words we speak, which reveal what is in our hearts, which lead to actions, and choices which determine life and death. Needless to say, the Christian must abstain from "all the appearance of evil" (I Thessalonians 5:22). In order to keep ourselves pure, we are reminded, "Do not let your mouth cause your flesh to sin" (Ecclesiastes 5:6, NKJV).

As a result of the increase in illicit sexual activity, the use of drugs, and involvement in witchcraft and other activities attracting evil spirits, people easily find cause to be unhappy. Whenever you have people living primarily to gratify the flesh, there is a higher risk of variance—contention, strife, fighting, discord, quarreling, and wrangling—whenever expectations are not met. Some people have been described as possessing the ability to "argue with a signpost."

Christians, on the contrary, are not to be given to quarreling or stirring up contention. Our Creator did not give the power of speech for the sake of argument. The power of speech is sacred, for He uses it, and He created it for His purpose:

> God, who at various times and in various places spoke in time past to the fathers by the prophets, has in these last days spoken to us by His Son, whom He has appointed heir of all things, through whom He also made the worlds (Hebrews 1:1-2, NKJV).

Made in His image to be sons of God, we ought to treat this ability to communicate as a holy privilege, to glorify Him, not to speak idly or in vain.

Some folks, however, are unaware or disdainful of the sacred, and cannot resist looking for opportunities to be controversial. They want to be the subject of conversations because of their controversial or outrageous behavior. But this does not speak of a right spirit. Among the things that the Scriptures state that the Lord hates, as an abomination unto Him, is "he that soweth discord among the brethren" (Proverbs 6:19). Creating discord is not a sign of a person controlled by the Holy Ghost.

Arguing for the sake of argument does not just happen; it usually springs from somewhere. We can describe its source in terms of "emulations." These entail fervent jealousies, envyings, and spitefulness, and refer to the wrongful desire to possess another's goods or possessions. This is the breaking of the tenth commandment, "Thou shalt not covet" (Exodus 20:17).

In our society, we do not lack for "crimes of passion," spurred on by a covetous nature. Class envy and class warfare also abound. Sometimes, these are even promoted for political purposes. Whatever the reason may be, words spoken out of a jealous spirit do not resemble those of a son of God. Whoever speaks such words is hindering himself from inheriting the kingdom of God.

The uncontrollable desire of the flesh is to get away from the laws of God at all costs. It is a flagrant disregard for right and wrong. This wild, unrestrained attitude toward life is what opens the door to lusts of all kinds. These lusts in turn will bring sin, and sin never fails to bring death (James 1:14-15). The soul that sins will die (Ezekiel 18:4). Finally, death will not be allowed into the kingdom of life, into the domain of eternal life.

Loss of Control

Another force that diminishes self-control is wrath. Wrath more specifically has to do with angry outbursts and fits of rage. People who cannot control their tempers are not manifesting the fruit of the Spirit, but rather the works of the flesh. They are not being ruled by the higher nature of the Spirit of God, but rather by the lower nature of sinful flesh.

Proverbs 25:28 says, "He that *hath* no rule over his own spirit *is like* a city *that is* broken down, *and* without walls." This work of the flesh makes the city liable to be conquered by its enemies. One who is ruled by wrath opens himself to being taken over by an evil spirit. Allowing evil spirits to enter, obviously, is not conducive to ruling in the kingdom of God.

And yet we are hindered by evil spirits more often than we know. They deceive us into thinking that what we are experiencing—anger, lust, etc.—is merely a product of our own thoughts and emotions, and is thus totally justified. In this way, we lose our grasp of what is sin. We need to realize that "the devil often speaks in the first person."

Selfish Ambitions

Strife, another tool of the enemy, basically has to do with contentions. It includes service of a party (as in a political party or a faction in an organization) solely to satisfy selfish ambitions. It creates the idea of a party spirit or partisanship, and is accompanied by untowardness (unruliness) and disobedience. This is Satan's way of gaining power, self-aggrandizement to the point of forgetting God; God's narrow way is that of self-effacement, loving God to the point of forgetting self:

> *But he who is greatest among you shall be your servant. And whoever exalts himself will be humbled, and he who humbles himself will be exalted* (Matthew 23:11-12).

It is interesting that the devil always moves in the opposite direction from what God would take. Some people are likewise filled with a contentious spirit. It does not matter what you say or what position you take, they will quarrel with you concerning it, taking the exact opposite stance. Again, this is not evidence of an abundance of the Spirit of God, nor is it a fruit of the Spirit. Contention is a work of the flesh, and as such, will hinder you from inheriting the kingdom of God and enjoying its benefits.

At the service of strife is a flow of seditions. "Sedition" refers to division, a standing apart, and dissension. When it is done in rebellion, sedition is the cause of church splits and often is the motivation of folks starting their own ministries, denominations, etc. They usually separate themselves because of something as insignificant as offended feelings, or not receiving enough attention.

Sometimes they separate because they do not have the political position or power they desire. So to appease their flesh (rather than overcoming it) and to "rectify" the situation, they start their own churches, denominations, or other organizations.

I do not mean to insinuate that all ministries and churches are started in this manner; many are led to begin by the Spirit of God. Unfortunately, division at times does come from sedition.

Evidence of a Right Spirit

Those that allow the Spirit of God to rule their lives produce certain results. Among these are the fruit of the Spirit, found in Galatians 5:22-23. The nine fruit of the Spirit—love, joy, peace, longsuffering, gentleness, goodness (kindness), faithfulness, meekness, and temperance (self-control)—are often interrelated. Indeed, you may have noticed that the word "fruit" is singular: this is because they have such a close relationship, each with the others, that they come as one fruit. Our words ought to cultivate each of these characteristics, both in ourselves, and in those who hear us.

The first of these is love. We do not refer as much to the feeling often associated with love; we emphasize love manifested as faithfulness, devotedness, and loyalty. First Corinthians 13, the Bible's extensive treatment on love, shows the interrelatedness of the fruit, with love as its head. For example, "Love suffers long, and is kind" (v.4), it "rejoices in the truth" (v.6), and faithfully "endures all things" (v.7).

With love comes joy, as in rejoicing and gladness. Joy includes both the feeling and the corresponding actions. Indeed, it is truly difficult to be full of joy and have no one to know about it.

He who loves, has peace. Peace has to do with more than just having peace with God; it includes peace with your neighbor. Truly, it does not just stop at serenity, tranquillity, and having a calmness in your spirit. It surpasses possessing peace of mind, or even displaying an even temperament. It is a peace that keeps you constantly in the presence of God while you love your neighbor.

Peace entails the ability of living in harmony with others. Someone with a peaceful spirit is easy to get along with; he will not likely be uptight, tense, stern, severe, or harsh. But the fruit of the Spirit is not equated with being easygoing on the surface. An easygoing person may not lose his peace very easily or "fly off the handle," but may still have difficulty getting along with others, which he hides so well you'd never know it. A person manifesting the fruit of the Spirit, however, lives in harmony with others out of a wellspring of inner peace. He exudes peace, love, and serenity. In order to send out peace, though, the results of our words should be peace and harmony. Jesus said:

Blessed are the peacemakers: for they shall be called the children of God (Matthew 5:9).

If we want to be the children of God, our words must produce peace. How is such peace gained, that is not betrayed by one's words, or upset by those of others? True peace is manifested through longsuffering. Longsuffering refers to patience in general. But more specifically, it refers to the patient endurance of evil and a slowness to avenge our injuries.

The apostle Peter beautifully illustrates the way longsuffering works. First, he told the servants to submit themselves to those in authority over them. He specified submission not just to the good and gentle masters—to whom it is easy to submit—but also to the perverse (I Peter 2:18). Then he explains longsuffering:

> *For this is thankworthy, if a man for conscience toward God* [because of his fear of God] *endure grief, suffering wrongfully. For what glory is it, if, when ye be buffeted for your faults, ye shall take it patiently? but if, when ye do well, and suffer* for it, *ye take it patiently, this is acceptable with God* (I Peter 2:19-20).

The fruit of longsuffering enables us to take our wrongful suffering with patience. We can take it in stride. Even when we are in the right, doing what is good, or standing up for truth, and we become persecuted for it, we will take it with patience. And we will have peace in spite of it. We still have harmony, a pleasantness about us, even if others are not, and will not be in harmony with us. We will manifest this fruit if the Spirit that rules our lives is the Spirit of God.

Longsuffering was manifested by the apostles when they were persecuted. They did not back down or compromise their message. Neither did they offer reprisal, verbally or otherwise. They chose to respond with a right spirit (Acts 4:18-20).

In longsuffering, or patient endurance, the sufferer appears somewhat passive, allowing himself, as Jesus, to be "done unto." Thus we offer no resistance to injury (Matthew 5:39), while still going about what the Lord wants us to do.

Kindness goes one step further: we are to *do good* to those who persecute us (Luke 6:29). The fruit of kindness draws our attention to action. Kindness that does not reach out and touch someone is not true kindness. For all the kind thoughts we may think, they do not help anybody unless they are communicated by word or deed.

Acts of kindness are what people need; no matter how small, they will seem large to the recipient. And when kindness is done to an enemy, God's power is present to change hearts. Even if the recipient of kindness does not respond immediately, a seed will have been planted in his heart.

Generosity

The Greek root word behind goodness means "profitable, generous and beneficent" (i.e., having a giving spirit). It refers to doing what is upright and virtuous. So goodness refers to a generous and giving person, as well as one who is upright.

Here is an interesting point about the "giving" side of the fruit of goodness, as well as the "giving" side of love. Some people, it seems, have a hard time giving tithes and offerings to God. Indeed, Martin Luther has been noted as saying that there are three conversions required of the believer—the conversion of the heart, the conversion of the mind, and the conversion of the purse.

During some law classes in college, the retired judge that taught our class would often quote one of his mentors concerning punishment and correction. "If you want to get to a man's heart, put your hand into his wallet and you won't miss it but by about that much," he would say while holding his thumb and index finger about a quarter of an inch apart.

Truly, if you want to get to a man's spirit, put your hand into his wallet and you will not miss it by much, if you miss it at all. Find out where a man's finances are directed, and you will learn much about where his spirit is directed. *"For where your treasure is, there your heart will be also"* (Matthew 6:21).

Not only are we generous with things, we are also generous with ourselves—our time and our words of kindness. We should not be stingy with a compliment. We should look for opportunities to say something positive, to catch someone doing something good.

I would like to draw the focus of our attention for a moment on the "profitable" aspect of the fruit of goodness as well as the "usefulness" aspect of the fruit of kindness.

Too "Heavenly Minded"

The statement has been made concerning some that they are "so heavenly minded that they are of no earthly good." This unscriptural statement clearly cannot be true. No one is more "heavenly minded" than God Himself. As Christians, we recognize that He, as our Father, is definitely of "earthly good."

To dispute this claim would identify one as non-Christian. To refute the idea of God being involved in the affairs of men, being of "earthly good," would be to place yourself in the camp of the agnostic way of thinking. Even the pagans believe that their gods are of "earthly good." That is why they pray to them.

In addition, no human being has ever lived that was more "heavenly minded" than Jesus Christ, "who is the image of the invisible God" (Colossians 1:15). He was God manifest in the flesh (I Timothy 3:16). He was the Word made flesh (John 1:14). He was from another world.

Not only that, but Jesus consistently talked about the kingdom of God or the kingdom of heaven. He was always talking about another world.

And yet, there has never been one of more "earthly good." We look at the life of Jesus and see where He made the blind to see, the deaf to hear, the dumb to talk, and the lame to walk. This is of more "earthly good" than most have ever aspired to being. This is so far beyond being of "earthly good" we might say that He was of "earthly great."

When Jesus walked on the scene, devils would be cast out of people. The stormy sea would be calmed. Folks would have their sins forgiven. Their shattered lives would be put back together again. Relationships would be restored. The hopeless received hope. Hungry crowds would be fed! Even taxes became paid! This is what happened when Jesus was around. Feeding the hungry? Paying bills? What could be more "earthly" than that? Surely, He was of "earthly good."

Spiritual Pride Reveals Spiritual Ignorance

This idea of being so heavenly minded as to be of no earthly good is usually applied to the Pharisees. But the Pharisees were not heavenly minded. Focusing on themselves and their reputations, their main interest was with their supposed spirituality and their show of righteousness. They were too carnally minded to understand the things of the spirit (I Corinthians 2:14).

Even one of the "most spiritual" among them was not able to comprehend the very basics of the kingdom of God. When Nicodemus could not perceive that Jesus was speaking of being born again in the spirit, Jesus expressed amazement that Nicodemus could not understand, though he was "a master in Israel" (John 3:1-10). Being born again is only at the basic level of heavenly things. Yet, Nicodemus could not grasp it. Their "experts" could not understand true heavenly things.

The truth of the matter is that the more heavenly minded you are, the more earthly good you will do. If you are of no earthly good, then you need to take another look at your "heavenly mindedness."

The fruit of the Spirit is goodness or profitability. If you are allowing the Spirit of God to rule your life, you will be profitable by helping people. Likewise, the fruit of kindness is useful. It is of earthly good.

Next, the fruit of faith has to do with belief, firm persuasion, being assured of the truth of the faith, and trust in God. It also entails honesty, integrity, and faithfulness. Not only that, but those that demonstrate the fruit of the Spirit will see the exercise of faith in their lives.

Our words should strengthen the faith of other Christians. They should be encouraged to faithfulness by our words. If we intend to encourage, but have the opposite effect on people, we need to ask God's help to direct our words towards His end.

The Strength of Meekness

Spiritual pride and ignorance are sources of weakness. Wisdom and true strength are what we find in the fruit of the Spirit known as meekness. Contrary to the thinking of some, meekness does not have to do with weakness. Some take the great promise of the meek inheriting the earth and turn it to mean that they will be trampled into the ground. That notion reveals spiritual ignorance: the promise to the meek is a grand one, that of gaining all the blessings of this life.

Meekness has to do with gentleness and kindness, modesty and humility. These attributes cannot come from weakness. They can only come from true strength.

If you are spiritually weak, you cannot fully express kindness, for you do not have enough of a source of strength to draw upon, so as to demonstrate your kindness ("You cannot give what you do not have"). If you are small and weak in the spirit, you cannot exercise true humility. You may feel humiliated, but that is quite different from being humble.

On numerous occasions, Brother Billy Cole has aptly stated that you cannot demonstrate true humility until you have been praised. Then you have the choice of responding either with arrogance or humility. There must be an initial base of strength to display the virtue of humility, rather than vice of pride. Virtues such as humility are habits: they are prayerfully acquired by achieving consistency in our actions.

True humility, or genuine meekness of spirit, enables us to keep our focus on God at all times. Constantly in close contact with the source of our salvation—our Savior—we can do what He commands, unhampered by distraction. Meekness enables us to obey the seed implanted in our souls, which has the power to save us (James 1:21).

Power to Control

Temperance has to do with self-control. If there is no strength or power to control, how can you manifest self-control? In fact, the meaning for *enkrateis* (the Greek root word behind temperance) is "strong, stout; possessed of mastery; master of self."[6]

There is a "restrainedness" of the individual who lives in the manifestation of the fruit of the Spirit. There is power to control the self. The individual is "in control." Or better, the Spirit is in control, or guides the person.

This is quite different from the wild, unrestrained lusts of the works of the flesh. The temperate individual is not ruled by the base desires of his flesh. He has control over the desires of the flesh.

So meekness does not have to do with being a doormat for people to walk over you. **Meekness has to do with how you respond when you are in a position of strength**. Temperance has to do with a certain reservedness about self. It concerns exercising mastery over the self, which includes exercising control over our words.

James told us to be slow to speak (James 1:19). Proverbs 13:3 says, "He that keepeth [or guards] his mouth keepeth his life: but he that openeth wide his lips shall have destruction." It is also said in Proverbs 21:23,

> "Whoso keepeth [guards] his mouth and his tongue keepeth [protects] his soul from troubles."

Having the fruit of temperance means that the Holy Ghost will work to help us control the words we speak. We will not speak uncontrollably. We will not speak every thought that passes through our minds. Remember, "A fool uttereth all his mind" (Proverbs 29:11). We are not to walk as fools but as wise men (Ephesians 5:15). This is evidence of the power of the Holy Ghost, for no man can tame the tongue (James 3:8).

In addition, those that demonstrate the fruit of the Spirit are not called to weakness and soft jelliness of lifestyle. They are not called to be passive "fuzz balls" that barely qualify as existing. Rather, they are told to "be strong in the Lord, and in the power of his might" (Ephesians 6:10). In fact, they are to be strong enough to master themselves.

In order to build up the kingdom, we must rediscover in ourselves and others the special dignity of our vocation as sons of God. This dignity is expressed in readiness to serve as Christ, who came not to be served but to serve (Matthew 20:28). But in order to serve others worthily and effectively, we must be able to master ourselves, or possess the virtues that will lead us into spiritual maturity.

Of course, this mastery of the self is not achieved through mere human willpower, but by being in touch with the Spirit of life. If we were to rely on human willpower alone, we would end up with a rigidity which is not the product of the Spirit of God at work. For where the Spirit of the Lord is, there is liberty (II Corinthians 3:17). Where the Spirit of the Lord is, there is a free-flowing of life.

The free-flow of the Spirit does not lessen righteousness; rather, the Spirit enables us to cultivate it. Remember, Scripture says that the kingdom of God is "righteousness, and peace, and joy in the Holy Ghost" (Romans 14:17).

The exercise of the power of God flows out of a righteousness built on faith. The mastery of self is a necessary part of this work. However, this process of building righteousness is is not meant to be a joyless torture, filled with anxiousness and fretting. With the Spirit as your "spiritual director," you will experience joy and peace.

It is a matter of balancing the power with the *purity* necessary to exercise that power in a way that does not endanger you spiritually. The Bible is *the* supernatural Book, totally devoted to the kingdom of God in power, and the New Testament is especially full of signs, wonders, miracles, and the exercise of faith. However, the epistles in particular are full of admonitions of what we should be careful to do—and what we ought to avoid—in that exercise of faith.

We must realize that a war is going on for our souls, especially as Christians. The enemy wants to tempt us, as he did Jesus,to twist our motives so that God's power will be used for unheavenly purposes. The flesh craves power, as does Lucifer. Only the Spirit can channel our zeal with wisdom. So, like David, let us pursue His righteousness first, trusting that God will give us all good things, including the opportunity to serve Him in the power of His kingdom (Matthew 6:33). (I will speak more about bringing the supernatural to work in our lives later.)

The joy and peace will come as we submit to the voice of the Spirit: we must trust that God will provide for us, that He will help us to forgive, and that He will strengthen us in the face of temptation. That is why, when the Lord taught His disciples to pray, He included the following in His prayer:

> *Give us this day our daily bread. And forgive us our debts, as we forgive our debtors. And lead us not into temptation, but deliver us from the evil one* (Matthew 6:11-13, NKJV).

Our words have decisive importance in our effort at self-mastery. Does our speech minister grace or sow seeds of sin to others? Do we lead them to, or away from, God? Do we offend others unnecessarily and so reflect a poor image upon ourselves? Do our vocalized beliefs, preferences, and opinions scandalize others, or do they affirm, giving people timely support and encouragement, from which they could really benefit?

Clearly, we must surrender our well-meaning intentions of bettering others, or our tendency to overly trouble others, and focus on our own salvation. The best way we can help others is by seeking to improve our own witness, and particularly that of our words. The Lord said that whoever loses his life (submitting the human will to His divine will, replacing our words and works with His) for His sake will find it (Matthew 10:39;16:25; Mark 8:35; Luke 9:24;17:33). For it is in giving that we receive; in releasing that we gain; in pardoning that we are now pardoned; and it is in dying, that we are born to eternal life.

This paradox of our human nature, that it must be denied in order to be truly spiritually fulfilled, is repeated too often in the gospels to escape our acting upon it. Let us then "die to self," or to the law of sin, and serve the Lord with our words, so that we reflect the newness of life, which can only be found in the Spirit:

> *Therefore, my brethren, you also have become dead to the law through the Body of Christ, that you may be married to another—to Him who was raised from the dead, that we should bear fruit to God. For when we were in the flesh, the sinful passions which were aroused by the law were at work in our members to bear fruit to death. But now we have been delivered from the law, having died to what we were held by,*

so that we should serve in the newness of the Spirit and not in the oldness of the letter (Romans 7:4-6, NKJV).

Self-mastery really does take place from the inside out. Jesus' message to the Pharisees was to clean the inside of the cup and dish, that the outside may become clean as well (Matthew 23:25-26). No one wants to drink out of a cup that is dirty inside, no matter how clean it is on the outside. Since we are transparent, in a manner of speaking, rather than emitting darkness, let us radiate God's light.

Let us submit our spirit to the Spirit, and our words will consistently conform, blessing others, and ourselves. We are to let our light shine in our speech, so that it "gives light to all *who are* in the house" [whether it be during family gatherings, church meetings, conversations with other Christians, etc.] so that they, in turn, "glorify your Father in heaven" (Matthew 5:15-16, NKJV).

[3]Kenneth Hagin, *Following God's Plan For Your Life*. Tulsa, OK: Faith Library Publications, 1993. p.28

[4]*Webster's New World Dictionary* (Third College Edition), Victoria Neufeldt (Editor in Chief), New York: Prentice Hall, 1988.

[5]Ibid.

[6]*The Analytical Greek Lexicon Revised*, ed. by Harold K. Moulton, (Grand Rapids, Michigan: Zondervan Publishing House, 1978).

CHAPTER SIX
THE POWER OF A WORD

Words Can Build or Destroy

In the exercise of faith, our words are of resounding importance for life and death. We need to avoid those that lead to death, and promote those that foster life. Words can be used to work destruction. Solomon wrote that "violence covereth the mouth of the wicked" (Proverbs 10:6,11). But they can also produce life: "The mouth of a righteous *man is* a well of life" (Proverbs 10:11). The righteous man is under the influence of the Spirit of life. Therefore, the product of his words will be life.

The well referred to in this proverb is one that springs up unto everlasting life (John 4:14, 7:38-39). Its source is the Spirit of life, the Holy Ghost. Therefore, as the spirit extends itself through the words of the righteous man, it produces life. Thus, "The mouth of a righteous *man is* a well of life."

But what comes out of the mouth of the wicked is violence, which works death and destruction. This is because the spirit behind the man is not a holy spirit. It is a wicked spirit. Therefore, its end is death.

Proverbs 11:11 says, "By the blessing of the upright the city is exalted: but it is overthrown by the mouth of the wicked." When the upright bless a city (blessings are usually transferred by the use of words), the city benefits by it. On the other hand, if the words of the wicked are prevalent in the city, the city will be overthrown.

Again, the spirit behind the words leads to blessing or curse, to life or death. The Scriptures teach us that "righteousness *tendeth* to life: so he that *pursueth* evil pursueth it to his own death" (Proverbs 11:19). The Spirit works to produce life, the eternal life God desires to give us. Jesus said that He came that we might have life, and have it more abundantly (John 10:10a). Meanwhile, our enemy seeks only our destruction, for he does not come except "to steal, and to kill, and to destroy" (John 10:10b).

Proverbs 12:18 states, "There is that speaketh like the piercings of a sword: but the tongue of the wise *is* health." Some people only seem able to speak words that hurt people. Everything they say seems to have a sharp edge to it. Their words are like the piercings of a sword.

Indeed, some of the people who are deemed comical always have an individual target or victim of their jokes. They always seem to take a jab at someone. I cannot believe this is good humor. What they are saying is hurting someone. Their words pierce like a sword.

We can list acquaintances, fellow workers, and even relatives, who are ready to say things so negatively critical of other people. All their words do is hurt people, cutting them down. They only point out the faults of others. They only see the negative. Their speech is like the piercing of a sword.

On the other hand, the tongue of the wise produces health. The words of the wise edify people. They do not stab them in the back. Their words build families, churches, ministries, and nations. Words indeed can be powerful and constructive.

Proverbs 10:20 says, "The tongue of the just *is as* choice silver: the heart of the wicked *is* little worth." The tongue, described by James as a little member and an unruly evil, contains great value in a just man. But the heart, which should be a man's greatest asset, becomes virtually worthless when it belongs to a wicked person.

The words you speak tell of what spirit you are, depending on whether they work to bring life or death. You may be able to hide the spirit that dominates you temporarily, by telling some lies. But you cannot do it indefinitely, because your words will soon bear out your spirit.

This is why it is literally impossible for news reporters to hide their bias or political or moral preference, even to set it aside for more than a fleeting moment. You cannot disguise a spirit. Though they are professionals, the spirit that is behind the dominant news media will make itself known at virtually every turn. Whether they try deceptively to hide their bias, honestly to set it aside, or do not hide it at all, they reveal the spirit dominating their thinking.

And the same is true for everyone, concerning everything we feel strongly about—politics, faith, morality, relationships, etc. We must continually resist divisive spirits which blind us to the truth, hinder God's power from flowing in our lives, and keep us from living in harmony with others.

The Power of the Spirit

The power of a word is no more powerful than the spirit that sends the word. Our human spirit has power. Of course it does not have as much power as the Spirit of God, for He has all power. It does not even have as much power as an angel, for we are made a little lower than the angels (Psalm 8:4-5; Hebrews 2:6-9). But the human spirit still does have power.

That is why there is a benefit from speaking positively to ourselves, and others. The power of a word to do good, and the effect that it will have, depends on the power of the spirit that sends the word. So we can do someone good by the words we speak, but we can do a person far more good if we pray, invoking God's Spirit. If we make His words our own, our words will carry God's power to heal, teach, exhort, encourage, and so on.

Sometimes the effect of a word does not strike you right away. The meaning of a word may take time to dawn upon you. That was the case with the apostles (John 14:26). Places, sights, sounds, smells—in short, circumstances—may trigger a happy memory, something we may have learned but forgotten, or a time of trouble. In any case, the words spoken on these occasions can have lasting effects on us.

Over a period of time, words can heal or they can kill. Proverbs 18:21 states that "Death and life *are* in the power of the tongue." Words can have decisive importance, even in a matter of life and death. There have been numerous instances to show that the effect of words spoken to individuals who cannot seemingly respond, directly or immediately.

Words that are spoken to people who are in certain conditions, such as being in a comatose state, seem to have an influence on them. We have heard of stories where death was consistently spoken to an elderly person. This, in turn, speeded their demise. Sometimes a spouse will not realize that their negative words are hurting their mate physically and otherwise. If patients are addressed with negative words, their chances of recovery drop. But if they are addressed with positive words, their chances of recovery increase. Many doctors encourage family members to speak positively to the patients, even to those in a coma, in an effort to help the recovery process.

Your tongue really is a key to a good life:

For he that will love life, and see good days, let him refrain his tongue from evil, and his lips that they speak no guile (I Peter 3:10).

The Condition of the Spirit Determines the Direction of the Man

Proverbs 18:12 says that "Before destruction the heart [or the spirit] of a man is haughty, and before honor *is* humility." But how does haughtiness bring about one's downfall?

Pride, arrogance, and haughtiness are trademarks of a spirit that exalts itself against the knowledge of God. These spirits work destruction; that is the only reason they make themselves known. They come "to steal, and to kill, and to destroy" (John 10:10). Therefore, when presence of these spirits is discovered, be assured that, without God's intervention, the lives in which they are found will come to destruction.

Remember, "the wages of sin *is* death"(Romans 6:23). "Evil shall slay the wicked" (Psalm 34:21a). "The perverseness of transgressors shall destroy them" (Proverbs 11:3b). "Sin, when it is finished, bringeth forth death" (James 1:15b). "The soul that sinneth, it shall die" (Ezekiel 18:3c). These, and many other Scriptures, bear out this truth: sin will work its destruction.

Conversely, before honor is humility. How does humility bring about honor? Humility is an attribute of the Spirit of God. God resists the proud while dwelling with those of a humble spirit (James 5:6; I Peter 5:5; Isaiah 57:15). As a result of dwelling with God, the humble will be given honor and glory.[7] Honor and glory are with the Lord. Therefore, those that dwell with the Lord, the humble, shall receive honor.

The Power of God's Word

A word is only as powerful as the spirit that sends it. God's word has tremendous power because the Spirit that sends it is the Almighty.

A word is the extension of the spirit that sends it. That is why the Word of God is so powerful. The Spirit behind it is powerful. In Genesis 1, God sent His Word to create our world.

When He spoke for light to appear, it appeared. When He commanded the waters to be separated, it happened. When He commanded the dry land to appear, it did. When He told the plant life to grow, it did. When He told the fish to fill the seas, the birds to fly, and the animals to walk the land, it happened in each case just as He said. In fact, the whole universe was created this way:

By the word of the LORD were the heavens made; and all the host of them by the breath of his mouth....For he spake, and it was done; he commanded, and it stood fast" (Psalm 33:6,9).

God merely spoke the Word and His Spirit began to work. **The Word of God was simply an extension of His Spirit; His Word was an extension of Himself.**

In the beginning was the Word, and the Word was with God, and **the Word was God***. The same was in the beginning with God. All things were made by Him; and without him was not any thing made that was made* (John 1:1-3, emphasis added).

God created the world by using His Word. His Word is powerful because the Spirit that sends it is powerful—all-powerful.

John goes on to say in verse four that in Him (the Word of God) was life. This is because the Word is an extension of the Spirit and the Spirit of God is the Spirit of Life.

Psalm 107:20 says, "He sent his word, and healed them, and delivered them from their destructions." How is a word able to heal and deliver? Again, the word is an extension of the Spirit that is at work.

So often, Jesus spoke only a word and performed the miracle needed, as did the apostles. Jesus told the leper, "Be thou clean," and immediately the leper became clean from his leprosy (Mark 1:41-42). Jesus told a man with a withered hand to "Stretch forth thine hand," and immediately, the hand was restored (Mark 3:5). He sent His Word and it healed them.

Jesus Equates the Word with the Spirit

Jesus also cast out devils by simply speaking a word. In Matthew 8:16, the writer records that they brought him many folks that were possessed with devils. Then it says that, "He cast out the spirits with his word, and healed all that were sick."

Later in His ministry, Jesus stated, "If I cast out devils by the Spirit of God, then the kingdom of God is come unto you" (Matthew 12:28). The word spoken was very simply the extension of the Spirit of God. Remember, "the Word was God" (John 1:1).

Whether you speak of His Word or His Spirit, you are speaking of the same thing, in a sense. His Word and His Spirit are closely related; they work or act together in the same action.

So also, when you speak of a man's word, or of a man's spirit, they are related. There is that sense of them being the same thing. Your words are an extension of your spirit. Consequently, when you speak, you alert the spirit world as to the condition of your spiritual man.

Distorted Spirits

Proverbs 15:4 says, "A wholesome tongue is a tree of life: but perverseness therein is a breach of the spirit." The Hebrew word behind "wholesome" is *marpay,* which refers to the idea of a medicine or a cure. The thought is one of bringing healing or deliverance. So a person who uses words to bring healing to someone (or ministers grace to the hearer) is a tree of life—a source of life, energy, vitality, and strength.

On the other hand, perverseness in the tongue is a breach of the spirit. Perverseness has to do with distortion. For example, in any given stereo system, distortion is what interferes with the hearing of a clear sound. The higher the distortion rate, the harder it is to understand what is being transmitted (or in the case of a tape or CD, what has been recorded).

The speakers of a stereo system can only handle so much volume before the sound becomes "distorted." This is especially true if there is not sufficient power to properly use the speaker. It then acts as if there is much static in the sound. The better quality of the sound has been lost. This is called distortion.

This distortion can be offset somewhat by providing greater power to the amplification of the sound. It can also be offset somewhat by finding a "cleaner" power source. This would be a power source that has a lower distortion rate.

What the speakers are to the stereo system, our tongues are to our spirit. It gives voice or expression to what is going on inside our spirit. Our tongues let everyone hear what is being "played" in our spirit.

Our lives should give out a certain sound. That sound should be definite and clearly understood. If our sound is distorted, it will only produce confusion. This hinders us from inheriting the kingdom of God. God is not the author of confusion, but of peace (I Corinthians 14:33)

If we are causing confusion among God's people, we are not being led by the Spirit of God.This uncertain sound ought not to be. James said that blessing and cursing coming out of the same mouth ought not to be (James 3:10). He did not say it could not be, but that it ought not be. We must get rid of the distortion.

If there is perverseness in our spirit, we will produce a distorted sound with our words and our lives. This can be done numerous ways. Distortion may come because the words we speak are untrue. In this case, the sound is distorted because something is wrong with our "speakers."

Distortion may also develop if there is an insufficient amount of power at work in our lives. In this situation, we need a greater power source. That greater power source is the Spirit of God. Jesus said that we would receive power after the Holy Ghost is come upon us (Acts 1:8). We need to get in touch with the Holy Ghost. We need more love, more power—more of the Holy Spirit in our lives.

Perhaps we might seem to have plenty of power, but still produce a lot of distortion (perverseness). In this situation, we need to find a "cleaner" power source, or we need to check our connections to that power source, which may be damaged or faulty. Our wires need to be repaired or replaced with new ones; this is the work of the Spirit.

It may be that the power source of our lives is not a pure spirit. Distortion may also come because the spirit that sends it is not pure. In this case, the "production" of the sound was of "poor quality." We need to check our spirit to make sure we are sending out the signals of a right spirit.

Or we may need to see that we are clearly receiving "signals" from the Spirit of God without outside interference. Perhaps we are being ruled by the desires of the flesh. When you are "between stations," you hear only bits and pieces of each if you can make out anything at all. We need to come into clearer focus, tuning out the flesh in favor of the spirit, like raising the base or treble.

We can also adjust the left, right or middle of your sound with your graphic equalizer, some of which are more complicated than others. Those systems used to control the sound quality at concerts, or to record and mix tapes, will have many more levers or indicators, and hence, much more precision. Whether we are simple or complex, we need to ask God to increase the sensitivity of our spiritual hearing. The impossible is possible for Him. He can adjust our "headphones" so that our spiritual ears can easily distinguish the voice of God from that of the enemy.

We may try to blend the sounds, as radio stations do, creating overlap or smooth transition from one song to the next ("good blends" or *segue*). But if we lack the proper sensitivity or "sound sense," and proceed under our own wisdom any way, we may encounter difficulty.

Abruptly changing styles, rather than utilizing similarities and variations between songs to make things go together well, will jar (cause them to disagree or be disconcerted) hearers more than anything else. Likewise, unless our words are consistent with the same source (the Word), and therefore possess the same Spirit, a mixed message will be sent, confusing the faithful.

If, however, we try to mix the sounds of the Spirit with those of the flesh, discord will result. The flesh strives to win out: it wants to be the loudest sound, the one that attracts the most attention. If we listen to it long enough, the flesh may become the dominant spirit in our lives.

Most types of music are diverse enough for us to distinguish the differences between them quite readily. But we must also be aware of more subtle distinctions between different types of sounds, which may reveal contradictions. The devil appears as an angel of light. Evil spirits mimic holy ones. Hence, it is possible to send messages that mimic, yet falsify the original, true one.

In the last analysis, distortion is like living perversely, in two different kingdoms, between two different kings. It can be likened to hearing two singers—which song will we sing? With time, and without prayer, distortion will lead to destruction. We do not want distractions or competing messages to crowd out the voice of God in our hearts.

If we rely on spirits other than the Holy Spirit, we will experience a breach in the spirit. "A breach in the spirit" has to do with a spirit that has been broken, crushed, or even destroyed. So when there is perverseness in our words, it produces a spirit that is broken, wounded, offended, or crushed. Of course, it may also mean disclosing a spirit that already is offended or wounded, and so wounds or offends others.

In contrast, a life that is led by the Spirit of God will not be full of distortion. It will not be full of perverseness, for it will not fulfill the lusts of the flesh (Galatians 5:16). For the Holy Spirit acts to purify our spirits, filtering out everything that does not rightfully belong to Himself. The more we rely on the Spirit who heals us, the more whole we will become, for His words heal. Our words then, will heal and bless.

Jesus told his disciples, "the words that I speak unto you, they are spirit, and they are life" (John 6:63). His words have a totally different effect on the spirit of the hearer: they do not wound or crush, but rather heal and make whole. His words produce eternal life.

Credibility in the Spirit Realm

We find the word "faith" 16 times in the book of James. It is found right at the beginning (1:3) and at the end (5:15). Furthermore, there are references to the results of faith (4: 7; 5:16-18), the fruit of faith (1:3-4,12; 5:7-8,10-11), and the evidence of faith (1:22; 2:17,26). James clearly wrote his book with faith in mind.

Though bound to confound some, James makes a case against things that destroy, undermine, or only resemble faith, without being the real thing. Notice how James says that some people use their tongue for both good and evil:

> *Therewith bless we God, even the Father; and therewith curse we men, which are made after the similitude of God. Out of the same mouth proceedeth blessing and cursing. My brethren, these things ought not so to be. Doth a fountain send forth at the same place sweet water and bitter? Can the fig tree, my brethren, bear olive berries? either a vine, figs? so can no fountain both yield salt water and fresh* (James 3:9-12).

We have stated that the word you speak is evidence of the spirit you have. Of course, if your words contradict your actions, you are a hypocrite. Hypocrites have no credibility, even among their friends.

You can only trust a liar to be a liar. You do not base your investment decisions on their word. You do not make career decisions on their word. You are even hesitant to accept their directions to arrive at a destination. You do not trust them concerning the little things, much less the important things of life. They are not trustworthy, and therefore have no credibility. Hypocrites have no credibility in the world of the spirit.

A spirit will send forth either words of godliness and righteousness, or godlessness and iniquity, depending on the kind of spirit producing the words. If the words we speak do not produce life, joy, and liberty, they will produce death, gloom, and bondage. It is no wonder the Bible has so much to say about the tongue and the words we say.

If our fountain sends forth both sweet and bitter water, it sends confused signals to the spirit world. Spirits on both sides will be unsure as to the spirit sending the word, and as a result, wonder on whose authority you are acting, or even whom you are asking to advance, or whom you are commanding to retreat.

Are we encouraging demons by our compromises at the same time that we invoke the Holy Spirit? Are we calling down, as James wrote, blessings *and* curses? This ambiguity, and incongruity, causes spirits not to listen as clearly, or take seriously, your spiritual authority.

If we are not attentive, we can easily lose our credibility in the spirit world, and will inevitably do ourselves more harm than good. We must learn to be consistent with the words we speak, so that they clearly denote which side we support, and of which spirit we are.

[7]See Proverbs 3:34-35; Psalm 75:6-7; I Samuel 2:30; Psalm 91:15; and John 12:26.

CHAPTER SEVEN
THE TREE OF MAN
The Fruit Reveals the Type of Tree

To discern of which spirit people are, we simply need to listen to their own words. In Matthew 12:34-35, Jesus said:

> O generation of vipers, how can ye, being evil, speak good things? For out of the abundance of the heart the mouth speaketh. A good man out of the good treasure of the heart bringeth forth good things: and an evil man out of the evil treasure bringeth forth evil things.

It is from the abundance of the heart, or from the predominant spirit of our innermost man, that we speak. If we have a good spirit, we will speak good things. If we have an evil spirit, we will speak evil things.

In the verse immediately before, Jesus spoke of making the tree good so that the fruit would be good. Else, we would be making the tree evil, with evil fruit. Either way, "the tree is known by *his* fruit" (Matthew 12:33).

The tree is our spirit. The fruit is, in part, our words. Perhaps this is where the apostle James got his illustration about the tongue being like a tree (James 3:12). Some try to make their spirit good by speaking good things. Their emphasis, like that of the Pharisees, is not beginning in the heart, but rather with the fruit.

We can try to carry out our good intentions, trying to make our words right. Many "positive mental attitude" activists do just that. But notice that Jesus' focus was different: He said that the tree must be made well first; the good fruit would follow. We must learn to make our *spirit* right with God, and the right *fruit* will follow.

Moses exemplifies the necessity of keeping your spirit right with God, so as not to allow bad fruit to accompany your speech. In Moses' situation, his impetuous spirit did not let him speak where, when, and what he should have. He was not able to enter the promised land because he disobeyed God's command to speak to the rock, rather than smiting it, to get the water for the people.

Psalm 106 talks briefly about this incident and talks about the root of Moses' problem. It says that "it went ill with Moses for their sakes: Because they provoked his spirit, so that he spake unadvisedly with his lips" (vs.32-33).

First, his spirit was provoked. Next, he spoke words he should not have spoken. Finally, since his tongue was the rudder to his ship, he disobeyed God's command. The result was that Moses could not enter into the promised land.

Moses was a very demonstrative person. Recall how he smashed the tablets on which were inscribed the Ten Commandments, when he came down from the mountain, and found the people in idolatry (Exodus 32:19). Very few of us can express righteous indignation or anger without sinning. Only Jesus, when He cleared out the marketplace from the Temple, could do so perfectly.

An impetuous nature and untamed tongue got Moses into trouble, just as they did Peter. Right after Peter's confession of faith (Matthew 16:16), Jesus had to rebuke him for not understanding the message or "folly of the cross"(I Corinthians 1:18). Instead Peter spoke with the "wisdom" of men (Matthew 16:21-23). Peter also denied Jesus with the words of his mouth (Matthew 26:70-75).

The Hebrews in Moses' time only had the Law, so there was no redemption for Moses which would have allowed him entry into the promised land. But Peter gained the opportunity, with Christ, to make up for the errors of his tongue. He had tempted Jesus to be the Messiah in a way other than God had planned, and ultimately apostatized, denying knowledge of Jesus and his being a disciple. He would struggle honorably for self-mastery, but not on his own strength, or by his own spirit, unaided:

"Not by might nor by power, but by My Spirit," saith the Lord of Hosts (Zechariah 4:6).

The human weakness of Moses and Peter reveal our need for the Spirit's guidance in perfecting the inner man, so as not to veer off from God's plan for us. It will be a process of exchanging our ways for His, but we need to start now, making our spirit right with God, so that good fruit will flow from us.

Prophets and Wolves

In order to make our spirits right with God, we should listen to the prophets God sends us. But how do we know whether a prophet is from the Lord? Jesus told us that we could identify the spirit of prophets, like we examine trees, "by their fruit":

> *Beware of false prophets*[if there are false prophets, there must also, of necessity, be true prophets], *which come to you in sheep's clothing* [they come with the appearance of being disciples of Jesus Christ], *but inwardly they are ravening wolves* [their spirit devours others as a ravening wolf]. [How would we know them?] *Ye shall know them* **by their fruits**. [Here we find the source for James' example of the tongue] *Do men gather grapes of thorns, or figs of thistles? Even so every good tree bringeth forth good fruit; but a corrupt tree bringeth forth evil fruit. A good tree cannot bring forth evil fruit, neither can a corrupt tree bring forth good fruit. Every tree that bringeth not forth good fruit is hewn down, and cast into the fire. Wherefore* **by their fruits** *ye shall know them* (Matthew 7:15-20, emphasis added).

A prophet is recognized by his fruit, as is anyone else. If his life bears the fruit of the Spirit and his words produce life, health, and salvation (eternal life), we know he is a true sheep. Of course, by his words we know his doctrine and can judge whether or not they are consistent with Scripture.

If his words produce the works of the flesh, ministering death and destruction to his hearers in the place of life and salvation, then we know he is inwardly a ravening wolf. He may have a *form* of a sheep, but his spirit is that of a ravening wolf: he works to bite and devour the people of God. His words produce death, rather than abundant life in his hearers.

In talking about qualifications of the leadership of the Church, Paul tells us that the tongue is an important characteristic. In I Timothy 3:2-3, he said that bishops must be vigilant (circumspect— cautious, discreet, prudent), sober (temperate, modest, humble, and of a sound mind—or "in his right mind"), and not a brawler (quarrelsome or contentious).

Paul wrote to Titus as to why bishops must know how to use their mouths:

> *For there are many unruly and vain talkers and deceivers, specifically they of circumcision: Whose mouths must be stopped, who subvert whole houses, teaching things which they ought not, for filthy lucre's sake* (Titus 1:10-11, NKJV).

In I Timothy 3:8, he tells us that deacons (literally translated, "those who serve") must not be "double-tongued." Even their wives must not be given to slander (v.11). If we followed Paul's guidelines, it is possible that some would lose their positions in the Church.

Older men in the Church also ought to be sober (vigilant, circumspect) and temperate (Titus 2:2). Older women are similarly instructed not to be false accusers or slanderers (Titus 2:3). But this teaching is not just for the elderly among us. Young men are exhorted to be "sober minded" (v.6), using "sound speech," for "that cannot be condemned" (v.8). Speaking words that cannot be condemned or reproved is a high standard to uphold, but one that is entirely possible with God's grace.

When Paul told Timothy not to let anyone despise his youth, he also instructed him to be an example to the believers "in word, in conversation [conduct], in charity, in spirit, in faith, in purity" (I Timothy 4:12). It is noteworthy that Paul gave first priority to Timothy's being an example in the words that he spoke.

Idle Words

Jesus stressed the utmost gravity of our words: our very salvation depends on them. In Matthew 12:36-37, Jesus said:

> *But I say unto you, That every idle word that men shall speak, they shall give account thereof in the day of judgment. For by thy words thou shalt be justified, and by thy words thou shalt be condemned.*

Why will we give account even of our idle words? They are indicative of our spirit. Once again, we speak from the abundance of our heart, from the overflow of our spirit.

If the words we speak produce fruit of righteousness, then we will be justified before God, and show our right spirit. In contrast, if our words produce unrighteousness, then by our words we will be condemned. Proverbs 10:19 says,

> *In the multitude of words there wanteth not sin: but he that refraineth his lips is wise.*

When we engage in many idle words, there will be no lack of sin. We will be sure to lapse into sinful conversation. Paul told Timothy to:

> *...shun profane and vain babblings* [empty and fruitless discussions]: [Why?] *for they will increase unto more ungodliness* (II Timothy 2:16).

Idle words lead us away from godliness, and thus, we lose the power inherent in godliness.

Could this be why James told us, "Let every man be swift to hear, slow to speak"? (James 1:19). Remember that we are to guard our words (Proverbs 13:3; 21:23). We are to pay close attention to the words we speak. We are not to walk as fools which speak all their mind (Proverbs 29:11), but to walk as the wise (Ephesians 5:15).

If you are a member of the Board for the "Gossiper's Grapevine," you need to resign. If you are a shareholder in "Slanderers, Inc.," you need to sell your stock. Some people take pride in their openness, saying, "I am known for speaking my mind." If this character trait refers to standing up for truth and righteousness, then it is fine. You can praise someone for their forthrightness. But oftentimes it comes across as bluntness, to the manifestation of an insolent or selfish spirit. Titus, however, reminds us of a better way, one that will spare us, and others, much grief. Speaking of the good seen in others, and refraining from detraction, results in the habit or virtue of sound speech:

> Sound speech, that cannot be condemned; that he that is of the contrary part may be ashamed, having no evil thing to say of you (Titus 2:8).

Christians are not to be known for tongues gone wild. Wagging tongues mocked Jesus on the cross (Mark 15:29-32). We should not speak idle (vain) words. Rather, we should speak soundly, so that no one can hold anything against us. Moreover, we should speak words of grace, blessing those who hear us (more on this in Chapter 12).

The Root of the Tree

In Matthew 3:10, we find John the Baptist preaching the need for purity of heart, saying,

> And now also the ax is laid unto the root of the trees: therefore every tree which bringeth not forth good fruit is hewn down, and cast into the fire.

Under the law of Moses, the emphasis was on the external. But with the coming of Jesus Christ, God was going to get to the root of the problem, "the root of the trees," the root being our spirit.

With Jesus, the Ten Commandments were intensified (brought inward), so as to reach our spirit. Jesus taught that the Commandments were more than mere prohibitions. Jesus brought in an understanding of the spirit of the Law. The spirit of the law beckons for a change in the condition of the heart, so that we will love God and neighbor in a way that hallows the Lord.

Living in the spirit of the law implies utilizing a new manner of "seeing," one that probes beneath the surface of things in our everyday lives. Seeing with spiritual vision means observing the possible reasons why things are the way they are, or appear to be. This perception looks more intently at the spirit behind things. Jesus had difficulty with the Pharisees because they did not see as God sees, but judged by outward appearances only:

> For judgment I have come into this world, that those who do not see may see, and those who see may be made blind...If you were blind, you would have no sin; but now you say, "We see." Therefore your sin remains (John 9:39-41, NKJV).

Under the law of Moses, committing the act of adultery was considered a sin punishable by death. But Jesus went to the root of the tree, directing attention to the problem in our spirit:

> But I say unto you, That whosoever looketh on a woman to lust after her hath committed adultery with her already in his heart (Matthew 5:28).

Not only are we not to commit adultery, we are not even to think about it. Not only are we not to sin against our wives, we are to love them like Jesus loved the Church—He laid down His life for her:

> Husbands love your wives, just as Christ also loved the Church and gave Himself for her, that He might sanctify and cleanse her with the washing of water by the word, that He might present her to Himself a glorious church, not having spot or wrinkle or any such thing, but that she should be holy and without blemish (Ephesians 5:25-27, NKJV).

Why is Jesus asking us to see as God sees? It is not so that we become overly scrupulous like the Pharisees, looking to perfect ourselves without His grace. He wants to be our source of holiness, so that we keep our eyes focused on Him for our salvation. Then He can show us what we are meant to be, and will be, in Him: "...We shall be like Him, for we shall see Him as He is" (I John 3:2, NKJV).

The first step is admitting that our vision is less than perfect—that we are not aware of spiritual things, and do not take sin as seriously as God does. Sin can be defined as falling short of the mark: "For we have all sinned and fall short of the glory of God" (Romans 3:23, NKJV).

It is amazing that the things we can see from the distance of 30 feet, a peregrine falcon can see from a half-mile. God wants to give us a similarly sharpened spiritual vision, as well as acute spiritual hearing, if we will only ask Him.

Peter fell inasmuch as he looked to himself, rather than the Lord, for guidance in critical circumstances. Peter began to walk in faith, approaching the Lord on the water, but started to sink when he took his eyes off Jesus, and looked at the wind and the waves (Matthew 14:30).

Peter cried out fearfully, "Lord, save me!"(v.31). His words, on the surface, spoke of Peter's need for physical salvation. But they also reveal the need of the man's spirit. The Lord then chided him, saying, "O you of little faith, why did you doubt?" (v.32). Our faith must be so ground in Him that we do not waver, but cling to our steady anchor. If we do falter, we must fall upon His mercy, which will not fail to catch us. That is why our Lord told Peter,

> But I have prayed for you, that your faith should not fail; and when you have returned to Me, strengthen your brethren (Luke 22:32, NKJV).

God wants to purify our faith, immersing us in His love, so that we can abide in Him at all times. Therefore Jesus said,

> Take My yoke upon you, and learn of Me, for I am meek and lowly in heart, and ye shall find rest unto your souls (Matthew 11:29).

In plowing fields, the oldest, most experienced oxen was usually placed with the youngest and most inexperienced. That way the strong ox shows the way, and pulls the majority of the load until the beginner comes to maturity. So it is with the spirit—His "yoke is easy, and His "burden is light"(Matthew 11:30). Likewise, we will be able to give the law its place, without being crushed by its weight. Paul taught us that the law is good, if we would use it properly (I Timothy 1:8). The Greek word behind good is *kalos,* which means rich, useful, profitable, honorable, and worthy of use. But to use it properly, we need the guidance and help of the Holy Ghost.

Under the law of Moses, the command was given that we were not to murder. Again, Jesus struck at the root of the tree when He said,

But I say unto you, That whosoever is angry with his brother without a cause shall be in danger of the judgment (Matthew 5:22).

Jesus uncovered the problem in our spirit, and exposed its end without Him—death. The apostle John said, "Whosoever hateth his brother is a murderer" (I John 3:15). With the coming of Jesus, the ax was laid to the root of the tree (Luke 3:9). God will probe our hearts, to see what we are made of:

Yea, a sword shall pierce through thy own soul also, that the thoughts of many hearts may be revealed (Luke 2:35).

For the righteous God trieth [purifies] the hearts and reins (Ps 7:9c).

The fining pot is for silver and the furnace for gold: but the Lord trieth the hearts (Proverbs 17:3).

We may wish that His sickle were not so sharp, or His light of truth, not so searching. But the purpose of His correction is one of mercy: He only disciplines or teaches those whom He loves (Proverbs 3:12; Hebrews 12:6).

Under the law of Moses, the law of God was written on tables of stone. But the people of God continually broke the covenant. They simply were not receiving it in their spirits. So the Lord spoke through His prophets of the days which were to come, in which He would make a new covenant, beginning with the advent of Jesus Christ, who baptized with the Holy Ghost (Matthew 3:11). This time He said,

I will put my law in their inward parts, and write it in their hearts (Jeremiah 31:33).

Instead of placing emphasis on the outside, and the things we can see, Jesus emphasized the spirit of man. He was going to change the spirit of man. He was going to change the tree and make it good, instead of just changing the fruit.

The tree of man had been corrupted in the fall. Though God had warned man from eating of the tree of knowledge of good and evil, man ate of it regardless. This willed disobedience corrupted man's tree. The spirit of man, which had initially been made in the image of God, was now infected with sin.

A tree gains its beginning life from its roots. So man's life comes from his root or his spirit. Because "the body without the spirit is dead" (James 2:26), God decided to have man "born again" of His Spirit:

> *You send forth Your Spirit, and they are created; And You renew the face of the earth* (Psalm 104:30, NKJV).

> *But when the kindness and the love of God our Savior toward man appeared, not by works of righteousness which we have done, but according to His mercy He saved us, through the washing of regeneration and renewing of the Holy Spirit, whom He poured out on us abundantly through Jesus Christ our Savior* (Titus 3:4-6, NKJV).

Rebirth of the Tree

Man had to be born again of His Spirit. Moreover, God promised that He would give to us out of the abundance of His Spirit:

> *And it shall come to pass afterward, that I will pour out my spirit upon all flesh; and your sons and your daughters shall prophesy, your old men shall dream dreams, your young men shall see visions: And also upon the servants and upon the handmaids in those days will I pour out my spirit* (Joel 2:28-29).

As human beings, we tend to focus on the external because we can see it. We avoid the internal, because we cannot see the spirit. Man looks on the outward appearance. The Lord looks on the heart, or the spirit (I Samuel 16:7).

> *Either make the tree good, and his fruit good; or else make the tree corrupt, and his fruit corrupt* (Matthew 12:33).

We naturally tend to want to make the fruit right so that we will appear well before men. But God desires to make the heart right, to make the tree good. God wants to internalize our vision, so that we will see the truth about ourselves, and what we can become, through His grace. The spirit must first be made right; then the right fruit will follow. The outside must not be neglected, but the focus must first be on the heart. Jesus said,

> *Cleanse **first** that which is within the cup and platter, that the outside of them may be clean also* (Matthew 23:26, emphasis added).

Changing the Nature of the Tree

John the Baptist preached that One mightier than he would follow. That mightier One who was to come would be the Christ, the Anointed One. Whereas John baptized with water, He would baptize with the Holy Ghost (Matthew 3:11). The One that was to come would make right the spirit, for He would give us a new spirit.

That was the wonder of John's introduction of Jesus—that He would be the One who would baptize us with the Holy Ghost. It was a revelation, an entirely new teaching to those unaccustomed to it, even though it was prophesied in the Scriptures. The Father Himself would have to reveal it to the people, as He did to Peter (Matthew 16:17).

We can try to make our fruit good without making the tree good. This is what the Pharisees were guilty of attempting to do. They were so conscious of making the fruit appear to be good that they neglected the heart. The fruit seemed good but their tree was evil. Their spirit was still corrupt. Inside, they were "full of dead *men's* bones, and of all uncleanness" (Matthew 23:27).

Scriptures clearly teach that "The heart is deceitful above all *things*, and desperately wicked" (Jeremiah 17:9). Without God's help, this is the condition of the heart of man. The prophet went on to record the words of God as warning:

> *I the LORD search the heart, I try the reins, even to give every man according to his ways, and according to the fruit of his doings* (Jeremiah 17:10).

With God All Things Are Possible

We must change the tree, the spirit of man. Contrary to many people's thinking, it is not impossible to change the tree. They claim it is all in the genes, that people are born with different traits that cannot be changed. They excuse some sins because, it is argued, the individuals were born that way. So to ask for change is impossible.

Yes, with man it is impossible. Some things seem to be set in stone. Some things are determined by genetics, and to us, may seem unalterable. Other things are the result of experiences early in life that seemingly can never be overcome. It appears that they will affect us for the rest of our lives. We are powerless on our own to change.

This is where many modern social programs and psychologists miss it. They are working to change the fruit without changing the tree, if indeed they are working for change that betters the individual. Sometimes they are simply seeking to justify the bad fruit. But we know you cannot change the outside effectively without changing the inside.

> For what I am doing I do not understand. For what I will to do, that I do not practice; but what I hate, that I do...But now it is no longer I who do it, but sin that dwells in me. For I know that in me (that is, in my flesh) nothing good dwells; for to will is present in me, but how to perform what is good I do not find....For I delight in the law of God according to the inward man. But I see another law in my members....O wretched man that I am! Who will deliver me from this body of death? (Romans 7:15-24, NKJV).

We cannot change the inside simply by human efforts. We need to bring God into the picture. The supernatural accomplishes what the natural fails in doing. Indeed, "With men it is impossible, but not with God: for with God all things are possible" (Mark 10:27). Only God's Spirit is able to subdue our flesh.

So we need outside help. We need a Higher Power. We need a new Spirit to make the tree good, so that the fruit may be good as well.

We may endeavor as hard as we may, trying to change the outside or the fruit, but if the inward man is not changed, it is all for naught. That is why we need a new birth. Remember, the key to a nature change is honesty. We must become honest with God and ourselves. We must be born again.

We must be born of the water and of the spirit (John 3:5). We must be born of God (John 1:12-13) for "whatsoever is born of God overcometh the world" (I John 5:4). If the fruit is to be made good, the tree must be made good. Being born of the Spirit, the Spirit enables us to act on the "law of God according to the inward man," giving us the power to do the things we should.

The Value of a Right Spirit

After Jesus was baptized by John, His Father said,"You are My beloved Son; in you I am well pleased" (Luke 3:22, NKJV). Jesus did what the voice of God wanted Him to do. He was led by the Holy Spirit. In Mark 9:7, the voice of God told us to listen to Jesus, and follow His example of pleasing God.

But if we do not know the law of the inward man, and are only led by the dictates of the flesh, we can not please God. If we attempt to serve God in addition to ourselves, or serve Him with a selfish motive, our efforts will not be blessed. At best, we will honor Him with our words only.

In the Old Testament, and especially under the law of Moses, the Lord grew tired of the people's efforts to make their fruit seem appealing, while the tree (their spirit) remained corrupt. The prophet Malachi warned the people, twice saying that they needed to "take heed to your spirit" (Malachi 2:15-16). Then in verse 17 he says, "Ye have wearied the LORD with your words."

What was it about their words—or the spirit behind their words—that so taxed the Lord's patience with them? The problem became clearer when Jesus came to earth. The people of His day would sometimes speak the right things, but their spirit still did not come to God. He quoted the prophet Isaiah to make clear to them the source of God's frustration, not just with them, but with the people of Israel, their forefathers:

> *This people draweth nigh unto me with their mouth, and honoreth me with their lips; but their heart is far from me* (Matthew 15:8; Isaiah 29:13).

Their words did not take heed to their spirits. This is why Jesus cried out in anguish:

> *O Jerusalem, Jerusalem, the one who kills the prophets and stones those who are sent to her! How often I wanted to gather your children together, as a hen gathers her chicks under her wings, but you were not willing!* (Matthew 23:37, NKJV)

Because they were not willing, God could not save them. A stiffened neck or hardened heart is difficult to heal, for it will not submit. This is why Jesus lamented, "How can you escape the condemnation of hell?" (Matthew 23:33, NKJV)

The Jewish leaders of His time would not be helped because it meant they had to change. They were content to give God what little they could, wanting to be all right just as they were. They were comfortable being above everyone else.

If only they could have emulated David, who was a true "imitator of God." David was one in whom the Lord delighted. He knew his need for God, and was not ashamed to admit his sinful human weakness. His prayed from the heart—with all his heart—and so God heard his prayer:

Create in me a clean heart, O God; and renew a right spirit within me. Cast me not away from thy presence; and take not thy holy spirit from me (Psalm 51:10-11).

According to Psalm 32:2, David understood the value of having a right spirit in the eyes of God:

Blessed is the man unto whom the LORD imputeth not iniquity, and in whose spirit there is *no guile.*

In Psalm 34:18, David provided great insight by saying, "The LORD *is* nigh unto them that are of a broken heart; and saveth such as be of a contrite spirit."

The Lord took delight in David, because David knew the value of attaining, and keeping, a right spirit. He knew the value of having a good root system to his tree: he put his emphasis on having a right heart with God.

CHAPTER EIGHT
THE SUBSTANCE OF A WORD

Honest Fishermen

In order to please God, it is not enough to have good intentions—our spirits must be in the right place. In order to see God in our midst, we must first know Him in the spirit. At key moments, something prevented the disciples from recognizing the Lord (Matthew 14:26-27; Luke 24:13-16). They did not know Him before, or after, His saving death and resurrection.

John places the following story in chapter 21 of his gospel, sometime after the crucifixion and resurrection of Jesus Christ, seemingly to emphasize how deep our love and faith must be in order to responsibly undertake the privileged commission to feed the Lord's lambs and tend His sheep (v.15-17).

A number of the disciples were fishing. They fished all night long and caught nothing. In the morning, Jesus was standing on the shore. However, the disciples did not recognize Him.

Jesus called out to them to see if they had caught anything for all their labors. "Children, have ye any meat?"(v.5). They replied that they had not. Jesus then told them to cast the net on the right side of the ship. They did as they were told and caught so much fish that they were not able to retrieve the nets again into the ship.

Assuredly, it is not as though the disciples simply fished on the left side of the boat all night. They were expert fishermen, having done it for a living. As any fisherman, and even a six-year-old amateur, would do, they fished on the left side, the right side, the front, the back, and perhaps even diagonally.

Not only did they cast their nets on every side of the ship, but they also must have moved the ship to different spots, to try to find a place where the fish might be drawn into the net. Undoubtedly, they moved the boat 50 yards when one spot was not working. When that second spot produced no results, they moved the boat 100 yards in another direction.

They must have fished all over that area, trying to find a place where at least one fish would end up in their nets. They needed to eat. They needed to make a living. Yet, all their efforts were fruitless.

Then came the first step to their miracle—they were willing to be honest. They needed simply to admit that they had nothing. Now if you know fishermen, they at least have to tell you the story about "the one that got away." The disciples, though, answered Jesus with a simple "No."

We must first be willing to confess to God that we have not always been profitable servants. Our efforts have not profited us at times in our work for the kingdom. Sometimes this is the hardest thing for us to do. It appears so difficult to confess that, on our own, we have often failed in our mission. It seems so hard to admit that we have fallen short of our goals.

We have spent much time and energy, trying to grow large churches and experience true revival, but we have little to show for it. Even though we have, in North America, the great tools of various types of technology at our disposal, we still have little to show for it. We have not made a strong enough impact on western society. We can search for strength, revival, and growth by our natural methods and never succeed. On our own, our results will be minimal.

Next, we see that what Jesus asked the disciples to do, in terms of skill or know-how, was not anything different from what they had been doing all night. Yet, they gained results once God became involved in the equation. Again, we can search for strength, revival, and growth by our natural methods and never succeed. "If all else fails, pray," is not a formula for success. If it is our policy, our results will be minimal. Prayer ought to be a "first opportunity" effort, not a "last chance" effort. But if we will be led by the Spirit, even what we have already been doing will be blessed. We will maximize our results.

The question is, do we honestly love and believe in the Lord to the exclusion of all else, so that He will say to us, "tend my sheep" and "feed my lambs?" The Lord chooses to give this privilege only to true sheep, as opposed to wolves.

Or are we simply interested in having a form of godliness, without having its power? Is it only important to have the right image, without having the right substance?

Image Over Substance

Today, in our society, we seem to be more concerned with image than substance. We can see this by the tremendous growth of the advertising and marketing industry. It is virtually impossible to avoid the media blitz that exalts image above all else. The marketing of products, companies, politicians, actors, musicians, models, sports figures, etc., is so important that it might be the determining factor for success.

If a person has the right image, chances are he or she might not have to work as hard to earn instant public adulation. The attractive or flashy need not do as much to be noticed, or to impress the outward-minded. They merely need to be "trendy," attractive, or lucrative, for a time. Truly our heroes or idols are of our own creation, after the image we want to raise up.

In the effort to produce, everything depends on the "packaging," or the outward presentation. It is solely a matter of doing enough of the right things in front of the right people. There is often no guarantee of character; this is not prerequisite, as long as the contract is kept on the terms agreed upon. Even if "the marketable item" gets in trouble with the law, "the show must go on," if at all possible. Economics seems to engulf all else.

We are often guilty of trying to cover up weaknesses, in the attempt to paint the marketable item with the strokes of "whatever will sell." We tend to work at putting the "right spin" on the latest events, instead of immediately dealing with the problems at hand.

Inevitably, we are more concerned about public relations than we are about honesty and integrity. Everything seems to be about "damage control." When the product is defective, the best type of damage control is to change the product, the company, the politician, or whatever else may be involved as part of the problem. If the substance is defective, we need to change it. But our society's answer is to do the best we can to disguise it, and just find the solution, quickly.

We also see evidence of our obsession with image over substance by the colossal size of the cosmetic industry. The sales volume of skin creams, hair care products, make-up, and even deodorants and perfumes seems to keep rising every year. People want to "look their best," however they may define it.

There may not be anything necessarily wrong with "trying to look your best" (though lines should be drawn, safeguarding against the lusts of the flesh). Some of the above items are even preferable, such as deodorants.

The issue is that, when there is a problem in our society, our solution is focused on trying to change the outward. It is not based on the attempt to change the inward man, or to develop character. Instead, its focus is to try to change the image.

Perhaps our goal is to gain better "self-esteem." It is worthwhile to note the consequences of gaining a better self-esteem by changing the image, rather than the substance. Not only will your new self-image be temporary, as images are, it is also a false sense of self-esteem.

We must not base our self-worth on anything other than the person of Jesus Christ. He shows us the value of our personhood; it was worth the shedding of His blood. We must avoid over-emphasizing the external, as if that was all that existed. When nothing is made of the interior of persons, the spirit goes unnoticed. It is spiritually unhealthy to think that human beings are bodies only, without souls.

Another sign of this misplaced priority of image over substance is evidenced by the weight-control industry. It seems that folks would rather take a miracle pill, go on some newly developed diet, or undergo surgery to lose the weight, than change their character, which is lacking self-control. It is much easier to do the former, than control your appetite and exercise regularly, which take discipline. We want to look healthy, but we may not want to exercise to do it.

It is difficult for the image-conscious to properly take care of substance, especially when it comes to the spirit. That is why our Lord wanted the disciples' full attention, if they were going to do His work. He implored them,

> Watch and pray, lest you enter into temptation. The spirit indeed is willing, but the flesh is weak (Matthew 26:41, NKJV).

Names

The image-substance contrast can be applied to our choice of names for our children. We do not typically name our kids based on the meaning of names, or after worthy role models. More often, we name our kids based on something that sounds good to the ear, or has the right initials. Of course, this is not wrong; it just seems to be the custom of the day. In the Scriptures, though, parents named their children based on a particular meaning. There was substance to the name. This, in turn, affected the spiritual realm.

Names often identify traits in people. They can reveal qualities about their character or their nature. Therefore, they can affect a person's life, if that person strives to emulate the meaning of their name.

In addition, when you speak a name, you are often calling for a particular trait. Remember, there is power in a word. A name calls for a trait. This is why Scripture puts such great importance on names of people, places, and even things (see II Kings 18:4).

The Effect of a Name

Looking back at the things that have consciously and subconsciously influenced my life, one of the most powerful influences was my parents' choice of my name. Giving me my name was probably one of the greatest things my parents did for me. They put much prayer into the naming of their children. They were also sure to name each of us after people written about in the Bible.

Given the name of David, I endeavored as a little child to try to emulate him. He was a man after God's own heart, so I desired to be a man after God's own heart. He was a man who displayed great courage, great wisdom, and great faith. So I desired to do the same.

When he sinned miserably and was confronted by the prophet Nathan, he humbly admitted his wrong and sought for a restoration of his relationship to God. So I have tried to do the same.

Growing up on the church pew, my attention was instantly caught when the preacher began to preach about David. I closely identified with David of the Scriptures, not only because we shared the same name, but it was he in particular after whom I was named.

A child will generally try to identify with the character of the person after whom he or she is named. Usually, they take on both the positive and the negative characteristics. This subconscious influence can often play a part, for example, as to why "Billy" grew up to be an alcoholic and a womanizer, just like his namesake uncle. Yes, names mean things.

We come to recognize this way of being through a similar or recurring type of personality, just as genes carry similar traits through generations. The "curse," or "blessing," of being a parent is that you often get a child just like yourself. Parents wish the same on their children, sometimes, for revenge or "poetic justice." This is humorous, but it is sadly true. So make sure you would like your kids to imitate your example: your response to God, your honesty, your sensitivity to the needs of others, the way you handle your anger, etc.

If we do not want our children to imitate our faults or bad habits, why would we want our children to follow in the footsteps of those we name them after? I do not know anyone who would name their child "Judas," after the betrayer of Jesus, or "Benedict Arnold," after the traitor to the American cause for freedom.

We do not want our children to grow up idolizing these personalities, and what they stand for. We certainly do not want them to take up their spirit of treachery, etc. We tend not to name our kids after cowards, but after heroes.

On the other hand, a child who has no meaning to their name (perhaps because it was made up, had a pretty sound to it, or started with the right initial) can be without a compass in life, as far as a name is concerned. Of course, direction can be provided by some other means.

Names Call for Traits

When you speak a name, you are calling for a particular trait. The name is the representative of the individual who owns the name. That is why the name of Jesus is so powerful. Jesus is the Almighty God (Isaiah 9:6). He always has been, still is, and always will be (Revelation 1:8).

Jesus was not just a human being. He WAS fully man. But He was more than that. He was God manifested in the flesh (I Timothy 3:16). The name of Jesus is so important because it represents the God of the universe. It is greater than any other name.

God also hath highly exalted Him, and given Him a name which is above every name: That at the name of Jesus every knee should bow, of things in heaven, and things in earth, and things under the earth; And that every tongue should confess that Jesus Christ is Lord, to the glory of God the Father (Philippians 2:9-11).

Jesus Christ was placed at the Father's right hand in the heavenly places,

Far above all principality, and power, and might, and dominion, and every name that is named, not only in this world, but also in that which is to come (Ephesians 1:21).

Not only were the names of people important in Scripture, but also the names of places as well. Great significance was attached to the names of places, and in particular, places hallowed by the Lord's presence. For example, the city named Bethel means "house of God."

The Bible also places much emphasis on the various names of God. These names tell us that God is our righteousness, our peace, the One who heals us, our provider, our shepherd, etc. They reveal to us aspects of the nature of God.

So names are important, if only because they are words. Words mean things—they stand for a substance and speak of the nature of one's spirit. They are also important because of the traits for which they call. Hence, for each name mentioned or cited in this book—David, Moses, Peter, etc.—we can think of personal characteristics, both strengths and weaknesses.

The Key to Changing Your Nature Is Honesty

Scripture teaches us that God is very interested in names. Jacob was determined to get a blessing when he wrestled with the angel. But before the angel would bless him, he asked Jacob for his name. However, by revealing his name, he would also be revealing his character or the trait for which he was known.

Jacob means "supplanter" or "deceiver." Jacob had to be willing to face who he was before the blessing of God would be placed on his life. He had to face the fact that he had lived life as a conniver, a liar. Only then could the blessing he sought for be given to him.

Before we can receive what we desire from God, we must be willing to face ourselves. We must honestly answer certain questions. Who are we? What are we really like (as opposed to what we like to think we are)? How do others perceive us? How does God view us? We must face ourselves.

We only deceive ourselves if we do not examine the way we have lived our lives. A false sense of self needs to be replaced by a humbler, truer estimation of self. We need to know ourselves in order to live.

This is one of the first steps of repentance: we must realize our sinfulness, our state of weakness, our inability to change. We must be honest with ourselves. This is the key to power with God.

Before the alcoholic can be set free, he must face who he is. Before the drug addict can be set free, he must face what he has become as a result of his own choices. The same goes for those in need of help with their marriage or other relationships. The same is also true for those who want to see miracles. We must recognize our own weaknesses before we can receive God's strength:

My strength is made perfect in weakness (I Corinthians 12:9).

God's strength is free to be manifested once we recognize our own weaknesses.

Who is able to dwell in God's presence? According to Psalm 15:2, we can only do so if we speak the truth in our hearts. We must come to a point of honesty, a moment of truth.

In the light of who God is, we will see what we have been, what we are like now, what we are not, and what we will be in Him.

In His presence, we cannot stand clothed in the robes of self-righteousness. God counts them but filthy rags. In spite of this, honesty with God and ourselves will open the door for the blessing we seek. Truth and honesty gives our words the proper substance.

"God's Phone Number"

On one occasion, I was preaching in a service where an agnostic was present. I think he had come to "get someone off of his back." After the service, I began to speak with him. When I referred to God, he said that he had never come in contact with God. Therefore, he was not sure that God even existed.

I asked him if he had ever tried to talk with God. He smugly replied that he did not know God's phone number. At that point, the Holy Ghost spoke to me to tell him that His phone number was "honesty." When I relayed that to the man, he arrogantly replied that it did not contain seven numbers. After I briefly considered it, I pointed out that the word, honesty, did have seven letters. When he realized that, he had no reply. God had answered his objection before he had even raised it.

If we want to come into contact with the God of the universe, and become an instrument to release His power, we must start by being honest with God and ourselves. Before our nature can be changed, we must be willing to face God just as we are. We will not find God if we are trying to put on a facade.

Once Jacob could face himself for who he was, and not for what he had convinced himself that he was, then the angel proceeded to change his name to Israel. *Israel* means "prince with God," or "one who exercises power with God."

When his name was changed, far more was changed than just a vocal or written identification. Jacob's character was changed. He became a new man. He would no longer be identified by the trait of being a deceiver; rather, he would be known as one who had power with the Almighty.

When his name was changed, his nature was likewise changed. Beforehand, he was not true to his word—Jacob even deceived his own father. Consequently, he had no power with God.

With his new nature, he started being true to his word. Therefore, he gained power with God. He left off being a deceiver or a supplanter, and became a prince.

When we are willing to face ourselves in all honesty, then God can come into our lives and change our character. Our character will go from being powerless, dominated by our sinful nature, to a place where we can exercise power with God. We can become the sons of God. We can rule over sin, instead of letting it rule over us and bring us to destruction.

Honesty is the key to a name, or a character, change. Truthfulness is the key to opening yourself to the power of God to see a nature change or a "tree change." Yes, you can change even your very nature, if you will start by being sincere with God.

The sinful nature ought not to reign or rule over us. If it does, it will force us to obey our lusts (Romans 6:12). If this happens, it can only mean our destruction (Romans 6:16, 21, 23; James 1:15).

However, once our nature is changed from being a slave to sin, to being a child of God, then we can be princes with God, the Almighty. As we grow in spiritual maturity and authority, we can begin to exercise power with God, for we gain entrance into the kingdom of God.

The Fountain of Man

But in order to be princes of the king, vessels through which He pours His power, we must first be the sort of vessels He can use effectively.

Solomon talked about death in terms of "the pitcher" being "broken at the fountain" (Ecclesiastes 12:6). The fountain comprises all that is involved in bringing water to you, from the source of water, to the water spout.

Man can be likened to a fountain. The tongue is the mouth of the fountain, from which the water comes. The heart, or the spirit, is the source of water for the fountain. The pitcher of the fountain is the vessel through which the fountain sends the water. It is like the fixture on the wall that we often call the "water fountain." That actually is the "pitcher." That "pitcher," or that vessel, is like the human body. Furthermore, one way the fountain sends forth "water" from its source is through the mouth. This is the picture of the fountain of man.

Just as the mouth of the fountain can only bring forth what comes from its source, so also our mouth will only bring forth that which comes from our spirit. From the abundance of our heart, the mouth will speak. So we must be careful as to what we take into our spiritual fountain.

Bitter Water

Jude 8 speaks of those that "despise dominion, and speak evil of dignities." Their spirit moves against authority, which is a representation of God. Their spirit moves in rebellion against God. Therefore, they oppose everything that is identified with God. Their fountain sends forth bitter water.

These people discount, and set aside, all authority as irrelevant. The result of their spirit moving against God, and all authority, is that they blaspheme and speak evil of dignities. What is in their heart becomes evident through their words.

Today, some still blaspheme and speak evil of dignities. Jude pronounces a woe on them (Jude 11), and says that the Lord will execute judgment on them (Jude 14-15).

Peter also spoke of people that have a wicked spirit. He spoke of them as those that "despise government." In their heart and mind, there is a disgust for authority. He goes on to say that "they are not afraid to speak evil of dignities" (II Peter 2:10).

Eight verses later, in II Peter 2:18, he describes them as speaking great swelling words of vanity, which are overly boastful lies. This, of course, is the same mind-set that caused Lucifer to fall from his lofty position in heaven (Isaiah 14:12-15).

Blasphemers speak words of boastful lying, evidence of the rebellious spirit behind them. They spew forth bitter water. Does a fountain give out sweet water and bitter? This would cause confusion, which is not of God. We would never know if we could drink the water of life out of this fountain. Clearly, this ought not to be the case with us.

Sour Water

Others murmur and complain about everything. Nothing can ever satisfy them. There is something wrong with everything. They are negative about everything. They truly are "sour grapes."

Paul told us, "Do all things without murmurings and disputings" (Philippians 2:14). He told the Corinthians,

Neither murmur ye, as some of them also murmured, and were destroyed of the destroyer. Now all these things happened unto them for ensamples: and they are written for our admonition, upon whom the ends of the world are come (I Corinthians 10:10-11).

Jude referred to Enoch's prophecy when he said that the Lord would come, with "ten thousands of his saints" (Jude 14), to execute judgment on those that were:

...murmurers, complainers, walking after their own lusts; and their mouth speaketh great swelling words (Jude 16).

It is not enough to put a "sweetener" in the mouth of the fountain: we want to change the source of water. We want to change the *nature.*

We are not interested simply in making an image look good. We want to change the substance to become pleasing to God, for He looks on the heart. More is required than simply changing some of the words we speak: our objective is to change the spirit behind the words. We are not interested in simply putting up an image of words that look good, appear right, or sound pretty or impressive: we want to have the right substance behind the words.

With all of this in mind, we want to pray with David the following prayer to God, who is able to help us, and redeem us when we fall:

Let the words of my mouth, and the meditation of my heart, be acceptable in thy sight, O LORD, my strength, and my redeemer (Psalm 19:14).

CHAPTER NINE
BOUND BY A WORD
Being True to Your Word

David's prayer, that the substance of our words be acceptable in God's sight, points to the fact that we are accountable for our words, which are vessels themselves, carrying power.

Psalm 15 talks about the kind of person able to live in God's "holy hill," in His tabernacle, where the glory of God dwells. Among other things, it describes one who "speaketh the truth in his heart" (v.2). If he is honest in his heart, we know that his words will be truthful as well, for "out of the abundance of the heart the mouth speaketh."

The Psalm next mentions "He that backbiteth not with his tongue...." Again, we see control over the words that proceed out of his mouth. What is more, it goes on to describe one who is so truthful and so true to his word, that he "sweareth to his own hurt, and changeth not" (v.4). The person that lives in God's holy mountain will be a man or woman of their word.

In Revelation 14, the apostle John mentioned "the hundred and forty-four thousand" (v.1) in the tribulation. He referred to them as people who were "redeemed from *among* men, *being* firstfruits to God and to the Lamb" (v.4), because of their honesty and integrity. They were set apart because "in their mouth was found no guile: for they are without fault before the throne of God" (v.5). These were people who spoke no lies; their honesty was intact. They did not speak words designed to mislead or deceive. In their mouth was no guile.

In much the same way, the early Christians were convinced of the gravity of their words. They took their words seriously: what they said, they did. Speaking something with words meant putting your whole being into what you did, or staking your very life on your veracity. Denying Jesus publicly then became an unspeakable offense. One could not apostatize lightly, without denying everything one stood for. Such a person continued living in the body, with the spirit of the man already dead. Such denials will catch up with you, sooner or later. Some Christians would, however, still take the cowardly route, paying pagans to renounce the faith in their name, not realizing that they did the deed just the same.

There was an unusual case, documented by an ancient historian, where a man was paid to do the very thing just mentioned, to deny the Lord in the place of another. But when the time came, the Holy Spirit must have met him on the spot, right where he was, for he instantly professed faith in God, knowing it would mean his death. He died, and his death triggered the conscience of the one for whom he had died, which resulted in that man courageously laying down his life as well. The power of the Word, even to the unbeliever, is mighty, for it is met by the Spirit. May we confess our faith as readily, without faltering, or hesitating.

We say God is bound by His Word; He must perform it. And He will perform it because His Word is an extension of His Spirit. His Word is He Himself (John 1:1 says, "the Word was God"). II Timothy 2:13 says that "He cannot deny Himself." He fulfills His Word absolutely, with unswerving commitment, every time.

God told Jeremiah, "I will hasten my word to perform it" (Jeremiah 1:12). He looks to confirm His Word. So we know that God is bound by His Word.

So Jesus, the Word of God, when the fullness of time had come (Galatians 4:4-5), swiftly brought us redemption, adopting us as sons. He obediently and zealously fulfilled everything written in God's Word concerning Him, even in the most difficult circumstances. He unflinchingly did whatever needed to be done, led by the Spirit of God. For Him there was no other way—it was "God's way or no way." Consider how He completely accomplished His mission in three short years. What a tremendous witness of constancy and fidelity His was!

Yet, knowing God's faithfulness, we, as human beings, **often will not be honest enough and truthful enough**, consistently, for us **to be bound by our own word**. We are willing to stand by our word until it is inconvenient, or until it starts to work against us. We want God to be bound by His Word, without making ourselves bound to our word.

But God dwells with those who stand by their word when it costs them, when something is spoken against their own "hurt." The tabernacle of God will include "He that sweareth to his own hurt, and changeth not" (Psalm 15:4c). Now notice what Jesus says in Matthew 5:37:

But let your communication be, Yea, yea; Nay, nay: for whatsoever is more than these cometh of evil.

Notice that Jesus said that if our speech loses its sureness and reliability, it has its origin in evil:

But above all things, my brethren, swear not, neither by heaven, neither by the earth, neither by any other oath: but let your yea be yea; and you nay, nay; lest ye fall into condemnation (James 5:12).

James writes that if we would not stand by our word, we open ourselves to condemnation. Undoubtedly, Paul lived by this code. He expounded on this truth as he wrote to the Corinthians:

When I therefore was thus minded [to visit the Corinthians again], *did I use lightness* [i.e., was I just kidding or "just throwing words"]? *or the things that I purpose, do I purpose according to the flesh* [according to what sounds convenient at the time or according to whatever my carnality may desire], *that with me there should be yea yea, and nay nay? But as God is true, our word toward you was not yea and nay* (II Corinthians 1:17-18).

Paul was careful in choosing the words that he spoke. There was a "restrainedness" to his speech. If he said, "Yes," then it was yes. If he said, "No," then it was no. This was so that his speech would be "yea yea, and nay nay." His actions were true to his word; he was not ruled by the flesh. So he did not open himself to the condemnation of which James spoke.

Now, the point of this discussion is not to get folks to be unbending and inflexible, unwittingly working out their own destruction as a result of words spoken in the past. Rather, we must learn to consider what we say beforehand, so that we will stand by our word:

Wherefore, my beloved brethren, let every man be swift to hear, slow to speak, slow to wrath (James 1:19).

If we will be swift to hear and slow to speak, we will find that we often also become slow to wrath.

Truly, **God is bound by His Word**. But if we want His Word to be even more effective in our lives, **we ought to be bound by His Word** also. Jesus told His disciples,

If ye abide in me, and my words abide in you, ye shall ask what ye will, and it shall be done unto you (John 15:7).

So we must be bound, both by our own words, and the Word of God.

God Speaks No Empty Words

God uses no idle (vain) words. When He said the words, "Let there be light," all of creation realigned itself to cause light to shine. These were not empty words. His words have an effect because He Himself is the Word; His Word is the extension of His Spirit. Therefore, things happen when He speaks, when He moves.

All the universe was formed by His word. He spoke, and it came into being (Psalm 33:6-9). All of His words work wonders because He is a God of wonders. His name is Wonderful (Isaiah 9:6), and He is full of wonders.

When Jesus spoke, His words were not unavailing. Things just happened when Jesus spoke. When He said, "Be thou clean," to the leper (Matthew 8:3), the man was cleansed from his leprosy and his skin was made brand new—as no skin cream could ever do .

When He said, "Go!" (Matthew 8:32), the devils had to leave. When He said, "Thy sins be forgiven thee" (Mark 2:5; Luke 7:48), sins were blotted out.

When He said, "Stretch forth thine hand" (Mark 3:5), a withered hand became as whole and useful as its partner. And when He said, "Rise, take up thy bed, and walk" (John 5:8-9), a lame man started walking, carrying his bed. God's words are not empty words.

When He said, "Peace, be still" (Mark 4:39), the raging winds of a great storm came to a standstill, and raging waves became as placid as lambs in verdant pasture. When He told a girl to arise, she rose from the dead (Mark 5:41-42). When he said, "Lazarus, come forth!" (John 11:43-44), a dead man came hobbling out of his tomb. His words accomplished what they set out to do.

Wonder-working Words

Jesus was the Word made flesh (John 1:14). Words came out of Him at every turn. On every occasion those words were powerful: they worked wonders. So even today, when He speaks, things are bound to happen.

Whether He pronounces blessings or woes, it will not return void. When He blessed the loaves and the fishes, they multiplied in people's hands (Matthew 14:19-20). When He cursed a fig tree, from the roots upwards it withered up and died, in less than 24 hours (Mark 11:12-20).

His blessings count. They are not idle words. They are not empty words. So when He says, "Blessed are the poor in spirit: for theirs is the kingdom of heaven" (Matthew 5:3), you and I have reason to look to the future: the kingdom of heaven belongs to us.

When He says, "Blessed are the pure in heart: for they shall see God" (Matthew 5:8), we have a reason to get excited. What greater promise is there than to see God?

When His Word says that He heals all our diseases, you and I can stand on it (Psalm 103:3). All of our diseases must disappear. And when He says, "Be ye sure of this, that the kingdom of God is come nigh unto you" (Luke 10:11), we have every reason to shout.

When He says that we have authority over all the power of the enemy and nothing shall by any means hurt us (Luke 10:19), you and I can have confidence in it. There is no greater protection than the strong tower of the name of the Lord.

When He says that certain signs shall follow them that believe, we can expect fulfillment. Why is this? It is because:

*...all the promises of God in Him are yea, and in Him Amen, unto the glory of God **by us*** (II Corinthians 1:20, emphasis added).

I have no reason to doubt His Word. He has never lied before; He will not start now. In the same way, the Word of God will not return void (Isaiah 55:11). It cannot return void because it is "part" of His Spirit. To say that His Word would return void is to say that His Spirit was not capable of doing the work. It would be a question of His power: it would constitute a doubt in His omnipotence. It would say that something indeed was too difficult for God.

The Word of God is not subject to amendment, modification, or rescission (the act of rescinding, cancelling, taking back, or making void) by man. It has been established, forever settled in heaven. Jesus said,

Heaven and earth shall pass away: but my words shall not pass away (Mark 13:31).

All of creation may falter, or cease to exist, but the Word of God will remain forever. His words are sure and steadfast. They will always come to pass—even if they have to work a wonder to do so. His name is wonder-full and wonderful is His nature, for that is His character trait. He is a wonder-worker and His words will work wonders.

CHAPTER TEN
THE FAITH OF GOD

Mountain Movers

Jesus said that our words will carry power, if we speak in His name:

> *Have faith in God. For verily I say unto you, That whosoever shall say unto this mountain, "Be thou removed, and be thou cast into the sea;" and shall not doubt in his heart, but shall believe that those things which he saith shall come to pass; he shall have whatsoever he saith. Therefore I say unto you, What things soever ye desire, when ye pray, believe that ye receive them, and ye shall have them* (Mark 11:22-24).

As we walk through life, we will encounter some mountains in our path. When the mountains appear in our way, we can make one of four basic responses. The first is that we can deny its existence. This, obviously, is pure foolishness, and will not get us very far. Others will recognize the existence of the mountain, but back off in fear. They will then complain about the mountain being in their way. At least they are being realistic. Even so, this response is still unprofitable.

The "positive mental attitude" people encourage us to be mountain climbers. They try to teach us not to be intimidated by the mountains in front of us. They encourage us to climb them. If that does not work, they exhort us to tunnel through it. This is progress: it helps you to get to the other side, for the mountain does not stop you.

But God has called us to go beyond even that—He has called us to be mountain movers. If we climb it, it may take us 40 days to get to the other side. Granted, this is better than letting the mountain freeze you in your place, so that you never reach the other side. But if we move it, it will only take us a small while to get to the other side.

The authority of a king is found in his word. The king does not doubt whether his commands will be carried out. He is confident that they will be obeyed. He fully expects his word to be carried out completely, to his satisfaction.

Likewise, we are to operate this way in the kingdom of God. We are called to reign as kings. We are called to be the sons of God. We should not doubt the Word in our hearts: we should have full confidence in seeing it come to pass. Our hope, when we are operating in the faith of God, will not disappoint us, nor make us ashamed.

Hope [when it is hope in God] *maketh not ashamed* (Romans 5:5).

Whosoever believeth on him shall not be ashamed (Romans 9:33; 10:11).

Confidence in Your Expectation

Jesus told us to "have faith in God" (Mark 11:22). The Greek phrase is *eckete pistin theoo,* which means to have the faith of God, or to have God's faith. From what does the faith of God come? What is the faith of God?

God is accustomed to telling the truth. He does not lie. The truth is that He cannot lie (Titus 1:2). Everything He says about life, morality, wisdom, righteousness, salvation, or any other issue is also true.

So everything that God says about the past is true. Likewise, whatever He says about the present—about any situation—is true. Therefore, whatever He says about the future must be true as well.

Even if, on the surface, it seems not to be true, it will show itself to be so. He expects it to become true. He can address things (problems, situations, diseases) that are not the way He would like them to be, and arrange them according to His satisfaction. He can call things, which are not, into being. Thus He can turn water into wine (John 2:1-11).

In a sense, the faith, or the expectancy that God has, is that whatever He speaks will come to pass, even if it may not be so before He speaks it.

God cannot lie; His words will not be proven false. When God said, "Let there be light," there was no light yet in our world for "darkness was upon the face of the deep" (Genesis 1:2). He expected His words immediately to be made true—which, of course, they were. So it is with all the words of God.

Jesus did not lie. Therefore, when He said, "Thy son liveth" (John 4:50), it could not be otherwise. The nobleman returned home to find that his son was no longer dead, or even dying, but healthy, and very much alive.

Jesus told the Syro-Phoenician woman to go home, for "the devil is gone out of thy daughter" (Mark 7:29). Up until that point, the daughter was still possessed. But once Jesus made that statement, the devil had to leave to line up with what Jesus had pronounced. He only spoke truth. So everything He said, He expected immediately to be made true.

The faith of God can often speak in the past tense because He expects everything to line up with His Word. When we exercise the faith of God, we can even tell a mountain to make its way to the sea, and it must obey. The faith of God expects all of His commands to be carried out immediately.

However, we put a hindrance to the operation of faith in our lives when we are not acquainted with telling the truth. We must learn to speak truth. A clear sound, free of confusion, will please any honest listener. But we may have to "develop an ear" for truth, or "fine-tune" the one we have, to receive it.

We must learn to line up with absolute truth. How can we make sure that what we say lines up with absolute truth? If we speak the Word of God, we speak absolute truth. The Word of God is infallible and inerrant. It is all truth. In speaking it, we open ourselves to receiving the faith of God.

Remember, "faith cometh by hearing, and hearing by the word of God" (Romans 10:17). Faith will come when we gain "hearing." We gain "hearing" by exposure to the Word of God (more on this in Chapter 13).

Adapt yourself to telling the truth. Then you can expect what you say to happen. That, coupled with the Word of God, is the faith of God.

Speak to the Mountain

Now, if we think that we can simply hear the Word of God without obeying it, and still exercise the faith of God, we will be unpleasantly surprised. For we put up obstacles to the faith of God when we do not line up to truth ourselves. We must be obedient to the Word. The apostle wrote,

> But be ye doers of the word, and not hearers only, deceiving your own selves (James 1:22).

Jesus said that if we had the faith of God, we could simply tell the mountain to be removed and be cast into the sea, and it would happen. But often this is not what we do.

Sometimes we look at the mountain in front of us and we wish it would move away. We pray that it be cast into the sea. We cry because it is in our path. We beg the mountain to move. We complain because it hinders us. We may even ask God to move it. But the mountain does not have an obligation to move until we speak to it.

If we truly believe, we will speak. The psalmist said, "I believed, therefore have I spoken" (Psalm 116:10). Concerning moving the mountain, Jesus referred to our speech three times in one verse:

> Whosoever shall say unto this mountain, "Be thou removed, and be thou cast into the sea;" and shall not doubt in his heart, but shall believe that those things which he saith shall come to pass; he shall have whatsoever he saith (Mark 11:23).

The reason the mountain may still be in our way is not because His Word is void of power. Maybe it is because we are void of speech. Perhaps we have never addressed the mountain itself—an action requiring outstanding faith.

We have prayed that God would talk to it. We have told everyone else about it. But we have not spoken to it. If you want the mountain to move, **speak to the mountain**.

I was in a service on the East coast, where I preached the power of speaking a word in faith. Afterwards, during the altar service, a woman near 50 years of age came forward, asking me to pray for her deaf ear: she had not been able to hear at all in that ear for quite a few years.

As I laid my hand on her ear, I felt the confidence of the Holy Ghost. I rebuked the deafness and commanded it to leave. When I spoke, I knew that she had been healed. I had complete confidence that she had received her hearing. Upon asking her, and testing the ear, we confirmed that she had indeed been healed. When you speak with the faith of God, you fully expect everything to line up accordingly.

But for faith in action to be classified as the faith of God, it must line up with the will of God. We could use all the faith in the world, but if it does not line up with the Word of God and the will of God for our lives, it is not the faith of God.

In being given the privilege, recently, of participating in the great revival in Ethiopia, I noticed how Brother Billy Cole spoke words of faith for healing, deliverance, and the outpouring of the Holy Ghost. These triggered the release of the power of God to do great things. As a result, blind eyes opened. Deaf ears became unstopped. The lame walked. The dumb talked. Crooked limbs were made straight. Devils were cast out. And many thousands received the gift of the Holy Ghost.

Rightly ordered, spoken words of faith line up with the Word of God. They are spoken according to the will of God. And they are released in the timing of God.

Faith Produces Obedience

Hebrews 11:8 says, "By faith Abraham...obeyed." If you truly have faith, you will obey the instructions from God.

Operating in faith is not like exercising simple mental calisthenics. If we truly do believe, then we will obey. Romans 16:26 refers to "the obedience of faith." True faith encompasses obedience.

Remember also the prophet Isaiah who, in prophecy about the coming of the Messiah, asked the question, "Who hath believed our report?" (Isaiah 53:1). Allow the Scripture to speak to you. The rest of Isaiah 53 makes references to Jesus' suffering. It would appear that He was not believed because His obedience included denying Himself, and picking up His cross—something we do not always want to do willingly. Even Jesus' humanity struggled with it, but submitted perfectly:

> *O My Father, if it is possible, let this cup pass from me; nevertheless, not as I will but as You will...O My Father, if this cup cannot pass away from Me unless I drink it, Your will be done* (Matthew 26:39,42, NKJV).

He is the head; we are the body (Ephesians 1:22-23). What should our response in faith be? The apostle Paul makes it a bit clearer when He says in Romans 10:16,

> *But they have not all obeyed the gospel. For Esaias saith, Lord, who hath believed our report?*

Believing the good news about Jesus Christ is equated with obeying it. **The gospel of Jesus Christ is not to be merely believed mentally: it is to be obeyed as well.**

We know that the greatest commandment is to love the Lord our God with all of our heart, soul, mind, and strength (Matthew 22:37; Deuteronomy 6:5). Jesus said, "If ye love me, keep my commandments" (John 14:15). He also said, "If a man love me, he will keep my words" (John 14:23). Furthermore, He said, "He that loveth me not keepeth not my sayings" (John 14:24). Surely, by their fruits you will know them. The Christian paradox is that true freedom is given to all those who obey.

In Luke 6:43-45, we find Jesus teaching about how we speak from the abundance of our heart. (Similar testimony is given in Matthew 12.) Then He said in verse 46, "And why call ye me, Lord, Lord, and do not the things which I say?"

Yet when you call Him "Lord," and do not obey His commands, you make yourself a hypocrite. Your words lie when you do this. Your spirit is not affirming that which is true. This causes angels and demons not to take your words seriously. Spiritually, you lose your credibility.

The believer does not just think that the Word is right—he obeys it. Kenneth Haney has stated, "A believer is more than one who would merely agree to the Word being true. A believer is always one who acts upon the Word of God."[8] Jesus said,

> My mother and my brethren are these which hear the word of God, and do it (Luke 8:21).

I was in a service in the Midwest where I knew a lady wanted to be healed of lameness in her feet. I also wanted to see her permanently made whole. During the series of meetings, I preached again about the power of a word, especially when it is sent by the Holy Ghost. At the conclusion of the service, I spoke a word of faith for the lame to walk. That lady obeyed the word of faith and began to walk. That night, she was able to walk properly, to the glory of God.

If you want to enter into the kingdom of heaven, you must *do* the will of God (Matthew 7:21). Just speaking the right words will not gain you entrance. There are no magical words in the kingdom of God, only right spirits. The right spirit will produce the right words, which will be followed by actions that produce results.

[8]Kenneth Haney, *The Anointed Ones* (Stockton, CA: Radiant Life, 1992), 73.

CHAPTER ELEVEN
WORDS GUARANTEED TO PERFORM
God's Words Get Confirmed

God confirms the words of His servants. The gospel of Mark says that the Lord worked with the apostles, "confirming the word with signs following" (Mark 16:20). The book of Acts tells us that He gave the apostles witness of the resurrection of the Lord Jesus with great power, or with great demonstration of His ability (Acts 4:33). The book of Hebrews supports this truth, saying that He bore them witness "both with signs and wonders, and with divers miracles, and gifts of the Holy Ghost, according to his own will" (Hebrews 2:4).

When we come to an interior place where we find ourselves reigning in the spirit, our words take on a guarantee. Our words become much more powerful: they become more sure, for they become confirmed by Almighty God. God bears them witness, even by working wonders. God's power especially flows when we speak with the faith of God. God has told us that He is the Lord that:

...confirmeth the word of his servant, and performeth the counsel of his messengers (Isaiah 44:26).

God will back up the words of the obedient communicators of His divine message. He will cause their words to take place. He will even reinforce their words when it comes to judgment.

After Elijah was taken up in a chariot of fire, Elisha went to Bethel. On his way, some children began to make fun of the power of God, telling Elisha to "go up, thou bald head" (II Kings 2:23). They made a mockery of Elijah, his mentor, being taken up. Elisha cursed them in the name of the Lord and two female bears came out of the woods and tore up 42 of them. Surely it is a dangerous thing to speak against the man of God, especially one by whom the power of God is manifested.

Death Pronounced

In Acts 5, we read an account of a husband and wife named Ananias and Sapphira. They wanted to join everyone else in giving to the church. At the time, there were many that sold their houses, real estate, and other valuable possessions and gave the proceeds to the church to further the gospel. (It would be wonderful to see people doing that today.)

This couple sold a piece of property, but decided that they wanted to keep back part of the profits for themselves. I do not think there was anything necessarily wrong with that. The problem was that they conspired to lie to the church, making everybody believe that they had given all of the money to the work of God.

They wanted to appear spiritual and dedicated to the same degree that everyone else was. That was not a bad desire necessarily. Desiring to be spiritual and dedicated is honorable. The issue was that they were going to lie to portray this image. They were lacking the substance. In other words, they were being hypocritical.

When Ananias came to lay the money at the apostles' feet, the Holy Ghost gave Peter a word of knowledge about the situation. Peter also discerned the spirit at work in this situation and he spoke up. Peter said,

> *Ananias, why hath Satan filled thine heart to lie to the Holy Ghost, and to keep back part of the price of the land? Whiles it remained, was it not thine own? And after it was sold, was it not in thine own power? Why hast thou conceived this thing in thine heart? Thou hast not lied unto men, but unto God* (Acts 5:3-4).

When Ananias heard this, he immediately fell to the ground, and died right on the spot. Some young men then arose, took him out, and buried him.

Three hours later, his wife came in not knowing what was done. Peter asked her if they had sold the land for the amount of money given. She affirmed that it truly was the case. Then Peter told her,

> *How is it that ye have agreed together to tempt the Spirit of the Lord? behold, the feet of them which have buried thy husband are at the door, and shall carry thee out* (Acts 5:9).

Then she also dropped dead instantly. No one took a sword to their bodies. No one fed them any poison. They were not in poor health beforehand, that this shock would give them a heart attack. Rather, Peter was speaking with the power of the Word of God, and what he said was bound to happen.

Blindness Pronounced

This was not the only case in the New Testament church when a judgment was placed on someone who fought against the kingdom of God. In Acts 13:4-12 we read the story of the apostles Barnabas and Paul trying to deliver the Word of God to a high ranking official, named Sergius Paulus. However, a sorcerer named Elymas "withstood them, seeking to turn away the deputy from the faith." But Paul, full of the Holy Ghost, said to him,

> O full of all subtilty and all mischief, thou child of the devil, thou enemy of all righteousness, wilt thou not cease to pervert the right ways of the Lord? And now, behold, the hand of the Lord is upon thee, and thou shalt be blind, not seeing the sun for a season (Acts 13:10-11a).

Immediately, Elymas became blind and left, trying to find someone who would lead him by the hand. The result of this wonder being performed was that the deputy believed and was converted. God will do whatever it takes to save us, teaching us by His Word to believe, act, and speak as we ought, so that we might show His power to those who have not yet experienced it.

Paul, being full of the Holy Ghost, needed only to speak the word and the judgment was carried out. These three scriptural instances show that there are two sides to the coin. Now the day will come, and even now approaches, when God will supernaturally defend His Church. When that time comes, people will be careful how they treat the man of God.

"It Is Enough!"

An older friend of mine told me of a time when he was a younger minister, preaching for a particular black bishop in Ohio, a pastor who was a powerful man of God. My friend told me that, at the time, this particular bishop seems to have had a number of problems with a certain woman, who had an evil spirit. She was not possessed, but her own spirit was so wicked and warped that she continually caused problems, interrupting services and calling attention to herself at almost every turn.

She came to a service one weekend while my friend was ministering at that church. During the Sunday night service, she began to stand up in the aisle and to scream and "do her thing." At that point, the tall elderly bishop stood up from his seat on the platform, stretched out his hand toward her, and simply said, "It is enough."

Immediately, she dropped to the floor, dead. The judgment of God had hit her as sure as it did Ananias and Sapphira (Acts 5). The result of the deaths of Ananias and Sapphira was that "great fear came upon all the church, and upon as many as heard these things" (Acts 5:11).

It is safe to say that the congregation had a tremendous respect for the old man of God, after the woman dropped dead in the church aisle. Most likely, anyone present would think twice before acting in rebellion, or speaking against the man of God.

There have been numerous like instances connected with the great Azusa Street revival, which took place at the beginning of the twentieth century. The same is true for various other places where there have been great movements of God's Spirit, such as the great revival currently happening in Ethiopia.[9]

"Look at Me!"

In the case of the death of Ananias and Sapphira, the Scripture states that,

Of the rest [of the people] *durst* [dared] *no man join himself to them* [the apostles]: *but the people magnified them* [esteemed them highly] (Acts 5:13).

They were understandably none too willing to claim such an impressive title as "apostleship." They dared not join themselves to apostolic service if they were not truly called to it. The power the Lord entrusted to the apostles was so great that it was fearful (Acts 5:11).

There are quite a few today that are only too happy to tag themselves with an honorable title, such as apostle or prophet, when they do not really have that calling, nor display its power. We are overloaded with people who are called to the glory of the pulpit, or the prestige of the platform. It has been said, "Some have been sent; others just went."

We do not need people who desire only to learn "which buttons to push" to win the approval of the crowd. We need men and women who are called to preach the gospel and to spread the kingdom of God.

Too many have been allured with their eyes to the grandeur of the office they desire, without having "prayed the price." They want the recognition of the title without the repentant state of the heart. They desire the fame without the humility. They crave the celebrity status that man can give, without walking the road of self-sacrifice. Their heart longs to be men and women of renown more than it desires to be men and women of God.

To be a man or woman of God requires time spent alone with God. The man of God must get to know His voice, His will, His Spirit, His Word, and His ways. To achieve "household name" recognition requires only marketing and advertisement. In other words, they must be involved in self-promotion. But God warns us not to touch "the glory," for that is His. Observe what happened to King Herod:

> *So on a set day Herod, arrayed in royal apparel, sat on his throne and gave an oration to them. And the people kept shouting, "The voice of a god and not of a man!" Then immediately an angel of the Lord struck him, because he did not give glory to God. And he was eaten by worms and died* (Acts 12:21-23, NKJV).

Just as in the case of Ananias and Sapphira, the result in Herod's death was that God was glorified, "But the word of God grew and multiplied" (Acts 12:24). The Lord will be glorified, in spite of our shortcomings. The question is whether whether we shall share in His spiritual glory:

> *Because God from the beginning chose you for salvation through sanctification by the Spirit and belief in the truth, to which he called you by our gospel, for the obtaining of the glory of our Lord Jesus Christ* (II Thessalonians 2:13b,14, NKJV).

If we die (to self) with Him, we shall also rise with Him (Romans 6:11). But we must realize that God's work is not to be taken lightly, for it has consequences attached to it, even in this life. Jesus Himself asks us, as He asked the apostles James and John, when their mother wanted the Lord to sit them at His right and left hand in His kingdom:

> *Are you able to drink the cup that I am about to drink, and be baptized with the baptism I am to be baptized with?* (Matthew 20:22, NKJV)

If we are willing to humble ourselves, and "pay the price" for being close to Jesus, we shall share in His glory, though probably not in the way that we would expect with our carnal minds (Matthew 20:23). Jesus glorified the Father by His life and his death (John 12:28, 13:31-32). As the head has done, so must His body. "Sunday" (His rising) only comes by way of dying. Even if we are not chosen to glorify the Lord with a martyr's death, we ought to do so by learning to die to self daily, that our new life in Christ might shine more clearly (Galatians 2:20).

Words that Do Not Fall

But if we will not submit, patterning our thought after His Word, we shall be "overthrown," and the power of our words will be brought to naught. We are told in Proverbs 22:12 that the Lord "overthroweth the words of the transgressor." In other words, God takes steps to render ineffective the words spoken by transgressors; He works to make their words useless, powerless:

> *Thus saith the LORD, thy redeemer, and he who formed thee from the womb: I am the LORD who maketh all things; who stretcheth forth the heavens alone; who spreadeth abroad the earth by myself;* **Who frustrateth the tokens of the liars, and maketh diviners mad; Who turneth wise men backward, and maketh their knowledge foolish** (Isaiah 44:24-25, emphasis added).

God works actively to undermine the words of liars. Here is another reason to be obedient to the Word of God, to be a doer of the Word: God will not let the words of His own come to nothing.

For the position of the transgressor is quite different from the position of the prophet, and in particular, Samuel. Of Samuel, it was said that the Lord "did let none of his words fall to the ground" (I Samuel 3:19). Samuel had his words confirmed by God Himself.

When Samuel spoke a word, it was bound to happen. It was bound to make an impact. None of his words fell to the ground. None of his words were rendered ineffectual. All of his words were confirmed, established.

Both Peter and Paul also had the Lord's confidence. They were astute enough to know that, if they pronounced death or blindness on an individual, it would happen. Their words would be substantiated, just as "the Word became flesh, and dwelt among us" (John 1:14).

So we can speak a word, knowing that it will be confirmed by God. Remember, though, that the great power God has invested in the

Church is not present so we can use it selfishly, being motivated by a spirit of revenge (remember James and John in Luke 9:51-56), or some other spirit. Power is there so that we can move effectively in accordance with the will of God.

Words Have Meaning

God counts a man's word to be of high value. Certainly, He would like to count on it. He told the people of Israel, in no uncertain terms, that they were to perform whatever they verbally committed themselves to God to do.

> *If a man vow a vow unto the LORD, or swear an oath to bind his soul with a bond; he shall not break his word, he shall do according to all that proceedeth out of his mouth* (Numbers 30:2).

In order to develop the faith of God, or to receive into our lives the operating power of the faith of God, you and I must first remove any hindrances, or points of resistance. We must comprehend how it is that words really do mean things—in the spirit realm. We must understand that we must quit saying things that are a hindrance to the operation of faith.

You have probably run into people who are always sick. They are always talking about sicknesses and diseases. They always are speaking of some type of syndrome or affliction.

They especially enjoy talking about the many infirmities they have. They can inform you of the latest diseases "hitting the market." They can list everyone who has died from your condition.

It is interesting that the modern medical profession has concluded that some people's sicknesses are all in their minds. They think they are ill from a particular sickness, so they confess it with their mouths. With time, they truly develop their sickness in their body. Psychosomatic illnesses are just that, brought on the body through the mind. People have claimed their conditions, and it came to pass just as they proclaimed. Oh, there is power in the words we speak.

Others always seem to be healthy. They pronounce words that produce health. They speak about health, life, and strength. They talk about "getting in shape." They articulate their goals in life. The words they utter have to do with progress and advancement. Thus, they get what they claim. Solomon knew what he was talking about, when he said in Proverbs 18:21, "Death and life are in the power of the tongue."

Psalm 103:5 tells us that one of our benefits in the Lord is that He "satisfieth thy mouth with good things; so that thy youth is renewed like the eagle's." God causes our youth to be renewed like the eagle's. One of the easiest, and most direct, ways He does this is through our mouth.

Is the Word "Ho-hum" to You?

Today, people often hear the Word of God preached, but it does not excite them. To them it is dead, dull, and dry. They view it as boring and meaningless because they have come to discount words, as if they had no value or power in themselves. So, in their thinking, neither does the Word of God have any value or power. They seem to believe that the only significance to the Word of God today is to teach a moral code, or to explain an after-death salvation. To some, it may produce the added benefit of offering some comfort in rough times, to provide an occasional inspiration, or even to lay the groundwork for theological or philosophical discussions.

But the Word of God is not limited to just these things. His Word works powerfully to accomplish His will. It is quick (life-giving) and powerful (Hebrews 4:12). It is our sword of the spirit; and as a spiritual weapon that we use, it is mighty (effectual) through God, to the pulling down of strongholds.

His Word is given to work the work of God, the work of the supernatural. It is spoken to change lives and to see things happen as a result. It was not designed to return void.

Proverbs 13:13 says, "Whoso despiseth [does not count it of great value] the word shall be destroyed: but he that feareth the commandment shall be rewarded." When you can internalize (take inward) that the Word has the power of the Almighty behind it, you will become excited about it being spoken. When you comprehend its connection to the moving of the Spirit of God, and that He—the Spirit—loves you and wants the best for you, you will be filled with anticipation of what He will say.

Furthermore, when you realize that He has given you promises for you to take to heart, promises that you can stand on, and that you can apply to your life, you will not sit there passively. It will make you excited about what the Word of God has to say. You begin to see how it will really work in your life.

Yes, there is reason to get excited when the preacher preaches the Word. When he preaches the gospel of Jesus Christ to us and tells us the promises of God, he is speaking words that are guaranteed to perform.

[10]Nona Freeman, *Unseen Hands* and *Then Came the Glory* (Minden, LA: Faith Printing Company, 1988 and 1994).

CHAPTER TWELVE
WORDS OF LIFE
The Body Ministers Life

There was once an unwritten rule, or "eleventh Commandment," that was initially heeded by members of the Republican Party in the United States. It stated, "Thou shalt not speak ill of a fellow Republican." I have heard it said that the "commandment" for a sports figure during a successful radio or a television talk show is, "Thou shalt not speak ill of thy teammates or coaches."

If Republicans could adhere to a principle of solidarity as a political party, how much more so should we, as the children of God, love our neighbor. If athletes can obey this principle for a sports show, how much more should the Church of Jesus Christ do the same. James 4:11 says, "Speak not evil one of another, brethren."

This does not mean that we should never speak a word of criticism. Criticism can be constructive, if offered in the right spirit, for necessary correction. But do we need to be consumed with words of evil? Must we be dominated with words meant for someone's destruction? These are not words of life. May I remind you that this tells us of what spirit you are. It is not the Spirit of God that brings death to the Body of Christ. Colossians 3:89 tells us,

> But now ye also put off all these; anger, wrath, malice, blasphemy, filthy communication out of your mouth, Lie not one to another, seeing that ye have put off the old man with his deeds.

Paul exhorts us to clean up our words. Get rid of that filthy communication coming out of your mouth. This is not only refraining from cursing, cussing, swearing, and using "gutter language," but also includes any communication that is not edifying.

While we are at it, Paul said we ought to be truthful in our communications. We ought not to lie to each other. In Ephesians 4:25, he wrote, "Wherefore putting away lying, speak every man truth with his neighbor: for we are members one of another."

Imagine if parts of our bodies began to send wrong signals to the rest of the body. What would happen if the nerves in the hand lied to the brain about the stove being hot? What if the hand told the brain that the stove is actually pleasantly warm? What would be the result?

What if your eyes began to lie to the body about what it saw while you were driving your vehicle? Talk about a brain that would soon go haywire! Of course, the body would soon also be destroyed.

If one member of the body lied to the other members, how would we know if a part of the body was truly hurt or in danger? There would be no way that the body could help that member of the body which needed help or nourishment. There would be no way of ministering to that part of the body. Not only that, but it would cripple the body as a whole.

The Body of Christ, or the people of God, is similarly connected, so that what affects one part, affects the whole. Our sins affect the whole body. We are not "only hurting ourselves." Every time there is a divorce, and especially when children are involved, we see that "we also hurt the ones we love."

If one part of your body is injured physically, you will not be as able to exercise the rest of the body until the wounded part recovers or is healed. You cannot run as fast or effortless with an infected toe. You cannot lift weights when you have a shoulder injury. If you try to do so, ignoring the pain, you will only delay the healing process. You may have the temporary satisfaction of getting in your workout, but you may have to wait even longer to fully recover.

It is difficult to wait to recover sufficiently first, before resuming the set of activities to which we have grown accustomed. We do not often like staying on "the sidelines"; we want to "get into the game."

But there are some things that must be attended to, when the "coach" calls for a "time-out," or sends in a "substitution" for you. Our wounds, physical, emotional, and spiritual, need time to heal. We may need refreshment, like a piece of watermelon on a hot afternoon, or a long drink of Gatorade. Or we may need to confess our sins, learn from our mistakes, and act more efficiently, giving less "fouls" or taking less "penalties."

The divine "Coach" cares for us far more than any earthly one, and He cares for our spirits with a lasting concern. Not only does He care for us individually, He loves us as His corporate body; He is concerned not only with our well-being, but also for that of our neighbor. As we are all His children, He wants us to be our brother's keeper

(Genesis 4:9), to love one another out of reverence for Christ (Ephesians 5:21).

How are we to treat one another in a way pleasing to Christ? We do so implicitly by our own example, but also explicitly, with our words. We cannot ignore the fact that, as human beings, one of our primary means of communication is through our words. We have a much more complicated life than do horses, for example, who cannot lie to each other.

We should be in the habit of speaking the truth to each other, as Paul wrote:

> *Therefore, putting away lying, "Let each one of you speak truth with his neighbor,* **for we are members one of another** (Ephesians 4:25; Zechariah 8:16; emphasis added).

In addition, Proverbs 4:24 says, "Put away from thee a froward mouth, and perverse lips put far from thee." Paul summed up how we ought to speak, with words that unite us in love, bringing life to the whole body:

> *We should no longer be children, tossed to and fro, and carried about with every wind of doctrine, by the trickery of men, in the cunning craftiness of deceitful plotting, but, speaking the truth in love may grow up in all things into Him who is the head—Christ—from whom the whole body, joined and knit together by what every joint supplies, according to the effective working by which every part does its share, causes growth of the body for the edifying of itself in love* (Ephesians 4:14-16, NKJV).

We ought to speak words that produce life, with Jesus as our example. He said, "The words that I speak unto you, they are spirit, and they are life" (John 6:63c). The words that He spoke produced life. In fact, all the words of God produce life for He is the Spirit of Life (Romans 8:2). "The Spirit **is** life" (Romans 8:10). "The Spirit **giveth** life" (II Corinthians 3:6, emphasis added).

Led by, and filled with the Spirit, our words ought to animate (give spirit and support) and encourage. We ought to edify, invigorate, and enliven those who hear us:

> *My son, attend to my words; incline thine ear unto my sayings. Let them not depart from thine eyes; keep them in the*

midst of thine heart. For they are **life** *unto those that find them, and* **health** *to all their flesh* (Proverbs 4:20-22, emphasis added).

"The word of God *is* quick [alive and life-giving]" (Hebrews 4:12). "Thy word hath quickened me [given me life]" (Psalm 119:50). We are called to be like Him: our words should also produce life. Peter said,

> *Wherefore laying aside all malice, and all guile, and hypocrisies, and envies, and* all evil speakings, *as newborn babes, desire the* **sincere milk of the word**, *that ye may grow thereby* (I Peter 2:1-2, emphasis added).

We are to cease speaking the wrong words, such as words spoken out of insensitivity or with deliberate intent to mock or injure ("killer talk"). Even if they are offered as humor, and are quickly apologized for, these poisonous darts, certainly have the ability to "find their mark" on our hearers, burdening them with weights that they are not meant, and should not have, to carry.

Instead of speaking out of ignorance—which is not "bliss" to our hearers—we are to pursue instead the "sincere milk (pure and genuine nutrition) of the word."

The term, "word," in I Peter 2:2 does not refer exclusively to the written word of God, although that Word is definitely included. The concept behind "word" (the underlying Greek is *logicon*) refers to the words we speak, as well as the thoughts or reasoning behind them.

Our words should not reflect a malicious spirit, or envying thoughts. Instead, our words should reflect thoughts that are nutritious to the spirit-man. They ought to produce health.

Words of Grace

Our words should be powerful words. They should have an upbuilding spiritual effect. They should not be as idle or vain words, which are useless, serving only to tear down. If we do not gather with Him, we scatter (Matthew 12:30). The apostle Paul wrote,

> *Let your speech be alway with grace, seasoned with salt, that ye may know how ye ought to answer every man* (Colossians 4:6).

Our speech is to be seasoned with salt. Salt will always have an effect. You do not put salt on meat, or any other dish, without it having some type of effect. So also, our words ought to be carefully considered, so as to have the proper effect on all those with whom we speak. Our words should not be so weak or vain that they simply "fall to the ground."

It also says that our speech ought to be always with grace. Grace is the power of God working in us, both to will and to do, of His good pleasure (Philippians 2:13). Our speech ought always to be laced with that type of power, seasoned with wisdom and temperance. It ought always to have a ministering effect on the hearer. Paul said as much to the Ephesian church:

> *Let no corrupt communication proceed out of your mouth, but that which is good to the use of edifying, that it may minister grace unto the hearers* (Ephesians 4:29).

Our speech ought to be such that it ministers grace to hearers. It is to minister that strength—that power to live the changed life—to the hearer.

Our words are to be useful for the edifying, or building up, of the Body of Christ. We ought to be wise, governing our speech to the building up of individuals in the Body of Christ. And you cannot edify the Body of Christ, without edifying individuals in the body, for His Body is made up of individual members.

Man, or the individual, is what makes up the Church: we must reach, or go through, him; we cannot affect the Church otherwise. And the perfect man, Christ, is our model and means to minister to all mankind:

> *And He Himself gave some to be apostles, some prophets, some evangelists, and some pastors and teachers, for the equipping of the saints for the work of ministry, for the edifying of the body of Christ, till we all come to the unity of the faith and of the knowledge of the Son of God, to a perfect man, to the measure of the stature of the fullness of Christ* (Ephesians 4:11-13, NKJV).

In addition, Paul told us to behave and speak in such a way, so as not to:

> *...grieve the Holy Spirit of God, whereby ye are sealed unto the day of redemption. Let all bitterness, and wrath, and anger, and clamour, and evil speaking, be put away from*

you, with all malice: And be ye kind one to another, tender-hearted, forgiving one another, even as God for Christ's sake hath forgiven you (Ephesians 4:30-32).

Our words must not be motivated by a bitter spirit. Instead, we must follow the example of love and mercy shown to us by God our Father. Because of Jesus' precious offering of His whole life in loving obedience ("giving until it hurts" or helps), the Father forgave us. We are to do no less: we are to forgive those who may have wronged or persecuted us, and offer nothing but love in return. Words spoken in this spirit cause our Father to rejoice, and open up the floodgates of His grace to all who will receive it.

Grace Is Power

Grace is not simply unmerited favor; it is power. The unmerited favor of God can be described as His mercy, which is "from everlasting to everlasting" (Psalm 103:17). The grace of God bestows unmerited favor to the point of providing power to help us. The writer of Hebrews said,

> *Let us therefore come boldly unto the throne of grace,* [why? for two reasons] *that we may obtain mercy, and find* **grace to help** *in time of need* (Hebrews 4:16, emphasis added).

Words that minister grace to the hearer provide an avenue for the power of God to help the individual. The author went on to state how grace assists us:

> *Let us have grace, whereby we may serve God acceptably with reverence and godly fear* (Hebrews 12:28).

Grace causes our words to accomplish something divine in our hearers: to serve God in a way that is acceptable to Him. Grace transforms us by infusing us with the reverential fear of the Lord, which is indispensable in serving Him.

> *The fear of the Lord is the beginning of knowledge: but fools despise wisdom and instruction* (Proverbs 1:7).

The more wisdom we gain in the fear of the Lord, the more power He can give us. This transition indicates the beginning of our form, godliness or reverence, being filled with dynamic power. With grace working this change in us, all the more should our words inspire others to live by the same grace, in reverence and godly fear. In this way, we help the hearer to live in a manner that is conducive to the fruit of the Spirit, instead of the works of the flesh.

> *For the grace of God that bringeth salvation hath appeared to all men,* [what does it do for us?] *Teaching us that, denying ungodliness and worldly lusts, we should live soberly, righteously, and godly, in this present world* (Titus 2:11-12).

Poor Stewards of Grace

We do not want to "waste," frustrate, or deny grace, the power of God working in us and through us. Therefore, we should be conscious about being good stewards, or good managers, of the grace of God. Peter exhorts us:

> *As every man hath received the gift,* even so *minister the same one to another, as good stewards of the manifold grace of God* (I Peter 4:10).

Brian Kinsey has stated, "We are the receptacle that holds the grace of God, and it is our responsibility to deposit this grace into the lives of every person we meet."[11] And one of the easiest ways that grace or power is ministered to people is through a spoken word.

You have heard that what we take into our spirit—what we read, listen to, or watch—can "fuel" a person's lifestyle. Such influence can move us in the spirit, or in the flesh, or both (distortion). Our words must not be used for corruption, or confusion, but must be used for encouragement, to build up the spirit in grace. We do not want to lose anything, or anyone, God has entrusted to us.

However, Jude prophesied that there would be those who would be poor stewards of the grace of God, who would turn the grace of God into lasciviousness (Jude 4). And there are people like this today, using a misconception of the grace of God to justify their actions, promoting the desires of the flesh.

Some people think arrogantly—that they can do anything they want to do without any repercussions. They use their liberty for licentiousness, permissiveness—as an occasion to have their lusts fulfilled. They believe that because they are "living in grace," they can live in lasciviousness. They fail to understand that lasciviousness is a work of the flesh, and that those that do the works of the flesh, "shall not inherit the kingdom of God" (Galatians 5:21).

Some people would also use the truth for hurtful means. What they say may be true, but it is designed to cripple rather than to produce life, health, and growth. These individuals need to be reminded of Ephesians 4:15, where it is written,

> But speaking the truth in love, may grow up into him in all things, which is the head, even Christ.

The truth spoken in love causes growth to take place. Our words should cause growth in the Body of Christ. Some speak the truth, but do it in a way that drives people away from the truth. We must speak with a right spirit, firmly but gently:

> With all lowliness and gentleness [meekness], with longsuffering, bearing with one another in love, endeavoring to keep the unity of the Spirit in the bond of peace (Ephesians 4:2-3, NKJV).

If we will not keep up the spirit of unity, bludgeoning others with the truth, we will be poor stewards of the grace of God, never releasing the power of the grace of God. In this case, we need to be hit with the truth ourselves. Being a poor steward of the grace of God would also include those who do not release the power of the grace of God through their lives. Being guilty in this manner would cause us to fulfill the parables that Jesus spoke of the servant who went and hid his talent in the earth (Matthew 25:14-30; Luke 19:11-27).

> I therefore, the prisoner of the Lord, beseech you to walk worthy of the calling with which you were called (Ephesians 4:1, NKJV).

> Let no one despise your youth, but be an example to the believers in word, in conduct, in love, in spirit, in faith, in purity (I Timothy 4:12, NKJV).

Words Used in Prayer

When we pray, we use words. Many have stated that "prayer changes things." Others have said that "often what ends up being changed is the one doing the praying."

The one, besides God, who hears everything we say in prayer, is our own self. So the words we speak in prayer are working to change us as we pray them, both because we say them, and because we hear them. Consider also that the words we use while praying also have an effect on the type of spirit we are developing in our inner man.

Also, praying the Scripture is one of the most effective ways to pray. Why? Because you are speaking what is the will of God. When you pray the Word of God, you are praying in the will of God.

When you pray in the will of God, you can rest assured that God will hear you and answer your prayer. You are speaking words that produce life, health, salvation, and answers to prayers. The apostle John told us of the confidence we can have when we pray according to God's will:

> *This is the confidence that we have in him, that, if we ask any thing according to his will, he heareth us: And if we know that he hear us, whatsoever we ask, we know that we have the petitions that we desired of him* (I John 5:14-15).

Jude admonished us, saying, "But ye, beloved, building up yourselves on your most holy faith, praying in the Holy Ghost" (v. 20). We are to build ourselves up in our most holy faith. What can be a more holy faith than the faith of God working in us?

Jude outlined the way in which we could build ourselves up on our most holy faith: by praying in the Holy Ghost. When we are praying in the Holy Ghost, we are speaking the words of the Spirit of God. Thus, we grow stronger, being built up on our most holy faith.

When you are praying "in tongues," you are speaking words of God that will not return void, but will have their desired effect. You are speaking the words of God, which work wonders. It is important to allow the Holy Ghost to have His way in our prayer lives.

"Let Every Chain Be Broken!"

I was preaching in Corvallis, Oregon, in April of 1996, when I made an altar call at the conclusion of the sermon. It was a Sunday morning service, and there were a few visitors present. Some of them came to the front, and we moved right in to our altar service.

As I moved in among the people, praying for them, I came to this one man who was kneeling and praying. He appeared to be of a mixed Hispanic descent.

While I was praying for him, I did not seem able to get a breakthrough. So I asked God for direction on how to pray for this man. I was looking for a word of knowledge or a word of wisdom. Although I asked, I did not immediately receive any answer from God concerning a word to give him, or a direction to follow in prayer.

Observing him kneeling, I knew that he needed repentance, so I began to pray in that direction. As I prayed, I continued to seek God for a word. All that I received as a response was to speak in tongues. I was already doing that, as any Spirit-filled person would do, so I continued to pray a while longer.

When I had nothing else to say, and did not know what else to do, I went on to pray for someone else. We had a very fruitful altar service. In fact, it was just about 3:00 in the afternoon when we left the church. Considering that the altar call was given at about 11:20 AM, it lasted quite a while.

After the man had finished praying, and while the rest of the altar service was still in progress, I went to speak with him. I knew he had not received the gift of the Holy Ghost as of yet, and I wanted to encourage him to continue seeking God until he was endued with power from on high.

While talking with him, I asked him a couple of questions. He let me know, speaking in very broken English, that he could not speak the language very well. I figured that meant that he did not understand what I was trying to say. I politely began to pull away when he stopped me, and said, "I—understand—aah—you—language."

I then thought that perhaps what I was saying to him, held meaning for him. So I continued to speak about the Holy Ghost. Again he stopped me, asking, "You—aah—speak—'nother—language?" I immediately thought that he was seeking a familiar language in which we could communicate.

He knew that I "look a little different" from the typical Anglo-Saxon appearance, something I had realized by often-asked questions concerning where I come from, or what my nationality is.

I replied that I could speak some Italian because of my parents. Other than that, I understood some Greek because of my studies in Bible college, but I could not converse in it, though I was willing to try.

I had also managed to pick up a handful of words in a couple of other languages, as most people do, but none that I could use in conversation. He shook his head, saying, "No, no. You—speak—aah—'nother—language."

Again I replied that I did not know another language. I was sorry, I apologized. I wanted to reach him somehow. At a time like this, I wish I had ordered one of those courses where you can learn to communicate in a language within sixty days by listening to cassette tapes.

He shook his head more emphatically. "No, no. You—speak—'nother—language. I understand—aah—you language." I looked at him quizzically. Very animated now, he spoke again: "When—aah—you pray—yes? Aah—I understand—aah—you—language."

At this point a little light went on in my head. Perhaps he understood what I was saying while I was speaking in tongues. As I talked further with him, I found this to be true.

This was later confirmed by his American wife and step-children. While I was praying for him in the altar service, I began to speak in tongues as most "prayed up" Pentecostals do. I did not know what I was saying, or in which language I was speaking. I was just trying to follow the Spirit of God.

He was from El Salvador, where the predominant language is Spanish. However, his family was from Brazil, where the predominant language is Portuguese. He spoke both languages well. But Portuguese was his familial language, the language used in the home for all private and intimate conversations.

While I was speaking in tongues, I began to speak in perfect Portuguese, without the slightest accent. He understood it and was amazed, especially when he knew that I had no knowledge of the Portuguese language. He even told me some of what I said.

Among other things, I had said, "I pray in the name of Jesus that every chain on this man be broken." Then I said it again even more powerfully than before, "I pray in the name of Jesus that every chain on this man be broken!" This was all later confirmed by his American wife and step-children.

I thought it wonderful, not only that God would do such a thing for this man, but that He would even choose the language most personal to the man. Only God is so thoughtful, so awesome. God knows how to speak to us most privately and intimately, so that we will listen to Him and want to do His will.

The next week the man came to the service where I was. Afterwards, he took the pastor, the pastor's family, and me out to eat. Actually, he paid the bill for the whole table of 13 people.

He told me that, for the rest of that day in which I had spoken in Portuguese to him, he could not eat a single bite—this coming from a man who had no problem with appetite. He also told me that, because of that experience with God, his whole body shook and trembled for the remainder of that day. God certainly grabbed a hold of his attention.

I have no doubt that every chain on that man has been, or soon will be, broken, because it was not I, but the Spirit of God, who spoke those words. Truly, I spoke in other tongues as the Spirit gave me utterance.

This was not the intellect of man at work, but the Spirit of God accomplishing His desire. And God's words work wonders; they will have results. They are not idle, vain, or empty words: they are words of life, grace, and power.

They will not fall to the ground: they will accomplish what they have been sent out to do. Therefore, when we pray "in the spirit," speaking in tongues, God will do great things. He will even reach people in the depths of their hearts, by speaking in a way, and a language, that is most familiar to them. May His kingdom come, and His will be done in power, through the words of grace heard from God, and spoken by His obedient vessels.

[11]Brian Kinsey, *The Bride's Pearl* (Hazelwood, MO: Word Aflame Press, 1993), 121.

CHAPTER THIRTEEN
USING YOUR FAITH

Jesus said, "He that hath an ear, let him hear what the Spirit saith unto the churches" (Revelation 2:7,11,17,29; 3:6,13,22).

By hearing the Word of God, we receive the ability to hear the voice of His Spirit. Faith comes by hearing (Romans 10:17). So speak, and hear, the Word of God.

You hear words, as well as speak them. Our faith comes by hearing, and hearing by the Word of God. If our ears are open to hear what the Spirit has to say, we can receive faith. For faith only comes by our hearing. Jude said that our faith is built up as we pray in the Spirit (v.20). When we pray in the Spirit, we do not only speak, but listen. Prayer is conversation with God, who loves us and speaks to us personally.

The fact that prayer is not a monologue, but a dialogue, is revelation. To the agnostic, even speaking to God directly is unfathomable. To say that God could talk back might send him shouting from the room. He lacks the proper context or background to understand how this can be.

The Word of God gives us the context as to how we can relate to God: it teaches us who God is, that we can come to know Him, and pray to Him. Furthermore, it teaches us how to pray, and how to listen to God.

We receive hearing by the Word of God. The Word of God helps us to "hear" from God. When we expose ourselves to the Word of God, we can receive hearing. When we have hearing, we can receive faith.

Jesus told His followers to "Take heed what ye hear: and unto you that hear shall more be given" (Mark 4:24). Jesus had been talking about the mystery of the kingdom of God (Mark 4:11-12). He told them that none of the manifestations of His kingdom would be hidden from them (Mark 4:22).

Then He told them to focus on what they were hearing. He said in verse 23, "If any man have ears to hear, let him hear." We are to pay attention to what we are hearing when we hear the Word of God.

I want to focus on what I am hearing. Moreover, if I do hear, then more is promised to me: "Unto you that hear shall more be given" (Mark 4:24). The fullness of blessings comes to those who hear. Through our hearing, we come to know God better. The more we know Him, the more we love Him, and want to serve Him. We find out how to serve Him, asking Him to reveal His will for our lives.

We must know the will of God, if we want to apply our faith to it. Faith comes by hearing, and hearing by the Word of God (Romans 10:17). When we know the Word of God, we begin to discern the will of God, and faith becomes activated in us. The Word of God tunes our spiritual ear to hear the voice of God. Hearing the voice of God, in turn, activates the faith of God working in us.

The Lord will use His Word to teach us the principles on which His kingdom operates. Then He will speak to us personally, by the voice of His Spirit; through others obediently speaking what they hear Him saying to you; and through circumstances that show, beyond the shadow of a doubt, that He is indeed with you. Within our lifetime, God gives each of us enough opportunities to get to know Him, if we are willing to look for Him.

Speaking Faith When You Have No Faith

In Ezekiel 37:1-10, the prophet tells of a vision he had, where the hand of the Lord carried him to a valley that was full of dry bones. The Lord took him on a tour of the valley, so that he could see how bad the situation truly was. He noticed that, not only were the bones dissembled from each other, but that they were also very dry. Those to whom the bones belonged had been dead for a long time.

The Lord asked him if the bones could live. Ezekiel replied that only God knew the answer to that question. Ezekiel was having a problem summing up his faith: he could not affirm that it was even possible for these bones to live. Regardless, he knew better than to say that it could not be done. He simply told God, "You know."

The Lord then instructed him to prophesy to the bones so that they would live. Ezekiel did as he was commanded. While he prophesied, Scripture tells us that "there was a noise, and behold a shaking, and the bones came together, bone to his bone" (v.7). Even after this happened, the miracle did not stop there.

The prophet reported that while he was watching, sinews and flesh came on the bones. In addition, skin covered them. Despite all of this, Ezekiel observed that "there was no breath in them" (v.8). They

113

were now simply a bunch of dead corpses. The valley was now filled with dead men.

This was progress from its prior state of being a valley of dry bones. Nevertheless, it was not of true profit. Ezekiel had obeyed. Yet, although he could not deny that some things did happen, he did not see a yield of profitable fruit.

Sometimes, we cannot deny that God has done something, but it seems like He does things that do not, to our way of seeing, result in fruit of any value. In a sense, our valley of dry bones has been turned into a valley of dead bodies.

Yet, this is not the time to condemn something as not being a work of God, nor the time to give up. What we need to do is see if God is saying anything else. He may not be finished yet. When He is finished, we will have fruit that is valuable. There will be "profit."

Speak to the Wind

Next, God ordered Ezekiel to prophesy to the wind. He was to prophesy that it would come, and breathe on the slain, that they would live. When he obeyed, the valley of dead corpses rose up to become a tremendously great army.

We notice that even though Ezekiel could not initially muster the faith to say that it was possible for the dry, separated bones to live, he obeyed God's command regardless (even if he could not see it). In other words, **in spite of his own lack of faith,** he still prophesied. **He spoke the words** the Lord gave him to speak, and the miracle happened.

We could learn a lesson or two in the operation of faith from Ezekiel. There may be times when we do not feel faith being active in our lives. But if God tells us to do something, the results will follow if we will obey.

If things do not turn out quite as gloriously as we had planned, we need to wait for God to speak again (and thus obey His voice again). If we do, we will see His great glory manifested. Place your faith in the God of faith, and watch the results.

Ezekiel did what he could, which was to prophesy. Then God undertook and did what He alone could do. God has a way of working in spite of our weaknesses. What is more, He will do it, if we are only willing to obey Him.

Dance!

I was in a service at a conference once, where the Holy Ghost began to move mightily. Indeed, the whole congregation, of about 20,000 people, broke out spontaneously in uninterrupted praise for over two hours, without any prodding from musicians, singers, or preachers. No one uttered a single word into the sound system to encourage any of this. They were waiting to introduce the speaker for the night.

I was sitting about halfway up in the balcony, praising God, while a number of people gathered in the altar area. After about 45 minutes of worship, I felt the Lord nudge me to go down to the altar area to pray for someone. At this point, I had no idea for whom I was to pray.

When I reached the altar area, the place was crowded. It was so crowded that you could not take a step without needing a person or two to move out of the way to make space for you. Even that was difficult, however, because there was no place for them to move.

After a moment, though, it seemed as if the crowd parted in front of me so that I could pass through it. No one had any idea who I was or why I was there. For that matter, I did not know what I was to do there. I was simply one of many. So there was no reason to make room especially for me. God was simply making a way so that I could get to the one for whom He desired me to pray.

When I came to the end of the path that had been made for me, there was a woman in a wheelchair. There were two or three men around her, praying for her. I had no intentions of interrupting their act of faith. I just began to pray with them.

Immediately, they opened up and allowed me direct access to her. For a moment's time, we prayed for a miracle, and then they lifted her out of the chair. She still was not standing on her own power. They had to hold her up.

In another moment, she was able to stand on her own power. At this point, I noticed that we had become the center of attention of some of the people standing around us. Feeling a little self-conscious, I managed to find a way to slip away.

I worked my way to the other end of the altar area. Along the way I prayed for several other people (two of whom received the gift of the Holy Ghost for the first time). When I reached the end, the Lord spoke to me to go back to the lady who had been in the wheelchair, and tell her to "dance before the Lord."

Once again, there immediately opened up before me a path to

walk through the crowd. Once again, it led me to the lady, who was now standing on her own power attempting to take a step. And once again, without their even knowing that I was a preacher, they opened up for me to pray for her.

When I reached her, I spoke rather softly to her in her ear (considering the noise of praise going up). I told her, "Dance before the Lord." God said, "Say it again." So I said it again. He said, "Say it again." So I said it yet again.

The more I said it, the more confident I became. The more confident I became, the louder I said it. The louder I said it, the better I felt. The better I felt, the more I said it. You can see the spiral effect of this, and understand that it wasn't long before I was shouting at the top of my lungs, "Dance before the Lord! Dance before the Lord!"

Well, she began to dance. The miracle had happened. God had healed her completely—she could walk. In fact, she could do better than that—she could dance!

This time the crowd around us, watching what God was doing, had grown considerably. I have to confess that again I became self-conscious. So, rather than stay and try to claim the "spiritual credit" for what God had just wrought, with His power, I slipped away. I knew that God wanted the glory for it.

The next time I saw that lady was about five or ten minutes later. She was up on stage, dancing before the Lord with another preacher (Brother Teklemeriam), and demonstrating what God had done for her.

Now I know that I was not the only person praying for her that night. There was great faith in action that night. I simply told this story from my perspective.

Here was a case where I did as I was told, and God did a work. The first work did not seem so profitable. But God was not finished yet. He said to speak a second time. Then He finished the work.

Use Your Measure

Romans 12:3 says that God has given to every man the measure of faith. We often read this as if it said "a measure of faith." Thus, we take it to mean that every individual has a different amount of faith given to him. But the Word says "the measure of faith."

It is not a question of how much faith you have. Rather, it is a matter of utilizing the faith that has been measured to you ("making the most of what you have"). Faith has been given to each of us. Jesus said,

If ye have faith as a grain of mustard seed, ye shall say unto this mountain, Remove hence to yonder place; and it shall remove; and nothing shall be impossible unto you (Matthew 17:20).

An old song, about a little bit of faith, said that we did not need a whole lot of faith—we just needed to use what we *did* have.

Now, you can use the faith that God has dealt to you to produce life, or you can use it to work death and destruction. You can use it in a positive way (the operation of faith) to obtain benefits or you can use it in a negative way (the operation of fear) and suffer the consequences.

Faith Versus Fear

Both faith and fear will produce: faith produces benefits, fear produces torment. We ought to have the kind of faith that excludes fear.

How do we get this kind of faith? Follow this progression closely: faith will activate God; God responds to faith (as opposed to need); faith works by love (Galatians 5:6); love is of God (I John 4:7); God is love (I John 4:8, 16); perfect love casts out fear (I John 4:18). So where there is faith, fear will not remain, for it will be cast out.

The apostle John wrote that "There is no fear in love; but perfect love casteth out fear" (I John 4:18). So there is no fear in God, for God is love. He that dwells in love, dwells in God (I John 4:16). So if you are living in fear, then you are not dwelling in God. God is love, and there is no fear in love.

On the other hand, fear likewise will produce its results. Whereas faith activates God, fear activates the enemy of our souls. Thus, fear brings torment (I John 4:18). Fear will produce death, bondage, misery, and sickness when it is allowed to operate freely.

In a crude sense, faith gives God the authority to act on our behalf, and to work in our lives. Fear empowers the devil to work in our lives.

Those who live with fear do not know peace. They are tormented every time fear is at work. They are tormented to their destruction.

Our God has not given us the spirit of fear, but rather the opposite spirit: He has given us the spirit of power, of love, and of a sound mind (II Timothy 1:7).

Faith activates the Spirit of God, who is also known as "the God of peace" (Philippians 4:9), "the Lord of peace" (II Thessalonians 3:16), and, "the Prince of peace" (Isaiah 9:6). Peace is part of the fruit of the Spirit. Where the Spirit of God is at work, there will be peace.

117

We need not worry about fear: as long as we keep our minds on Him, He will keep us in perfect peace (Isaiah 26:3); the abundance of our thoughts, heart, and spirit will be filled with Him.

Are You Praying in Faith or Fear?

I have noticed that the Bible does not mention the "prayer of fear." However, it does refer to the "prayer of faith" (James 5:15). The prayer of faith will bring results.

Sometimes we do not receive answers to prayers, because we are praying in fear, when we should be praying in faith. We hear about a particular problem and, in fear, we turn to God, because we are afraid. But we should *always* be ready to turn to God.

In Matthew 14, we recount the disciples' memorable encounter with Jesus walking on the water. After hours of rowing throughout the night, the disciples looked and saw Jesus coming to them. They thought it was a spirit.

Then the writer tells us that they cried out for fear. Jesus responded by telling them to be of good cheer. Although they heard His voice and received comfort from it, they still were not able to participate in the supernatural, because they were not using their faith. They received comfort, but did not yet receive a miracle.

Then Peter decided that he wanted to walk on the water. He asked Jesus to let him do so, and of course, Jesus told him to come. As long as Peter decided to exercise his faith, he was able to participate in the supernatural. But when he lived in fear, he could not do what Jesus was doing.

When we are moved by fear, we may receive comfort from God because He loves us, but we will not be able to participate in God's supernatural plan for us. On the other hand, when we respond with faith, we open the door to all that God has for us supernaturally.

If our faith in God is limited by circumstances, we will believe, but that belief will not express itself in power. We may as well sit tight in the boat, where it is comfortable, safe—never taking the risk of stepping out in faith. In that case, we might ask, "what kind of faith is it?"

Check Your Love Level

Faith that cracks under pressure is certainly not the kind the Lord had in mind; He did not become man, spending all that time with us, for that feeble result. Jesus answers this question when He said to

Peter, "O you of little faith, why did you doubt?"(v.31). Is it any wonder, after the resurrection, that Jesus asked Peter three times if he loved Him? (John 21:15-17)

There is a connection between faith and love. It is known as hope, or trust. The three are linked, mentioned together in I Corinthians 13:13: "And now abide faith, hope, love, these three; but the greatest of these *is* love."

We are not called just to have faith, but to love what we believe. We are to receive "the love of the truth" (II Thessalonians 2:10). That is why God gave us the gospel, for in it we find the strength to move in trust from one level of belief to another, or "from faith to faith," all the while increasing in the power of God unto salvation (Romans 1:16-17).

Upon the death of Jairus' daughter, Jesus said that he was not to fear, because fear is useless—what is needed is trust (Mark 5:36; Luke 8:50). Imperfect belief, or the lack of trust, is also why Jesus scolded Thomas, when He appeared to the apostles in the upper room, telling him not to persist in his faithlessness, but to believe (John 20:27). If he really loved Jesus at that moment, he would not have doubted Him, for love "believeth all things" (I Corinthians 13:7).

Our faith will have results if we walk in perfect love, without fear. For fear indicates a defect or inability to love. When we truly love Someone, we trust Him. We do what He asks, without doubting His ability to complete a work, once He has begun it (Philippians 1:6).

Galatians 5:6 says that faith works by love. To the degree that love is at work, faith will be at work also. If you want the operation of perfect faith in your life, then operate perfect love.

When you have that perfect love, you will have the perfected faith you seek. We ought to ask why we do not see, in our western world, the great results of the operation of faith, while certain other countries do. Perhaps the answer lies in obtaining a more perfected love.

Kinsey has stated, "The fragrance of true faith in Jesus as Lord and Savior must prevail in our lives, and we will express that faith by showing love to all the saints. If the love is not present, the profession of faith is a lie. Faith and love are interdependent."[12]

To operate the faith of God, release the love of God.

[12]Brian Kinsey, *The Bride's Pearl* (Hazelwood, MO: Word Aflame Press, 1993), 107.

CHAPTER FOURTEEN
THE KINGDOM IN A SEED
Seeds Reproduce Their Own Kind

When God created the earth, He commanded the herbs and trees to bring forth fruit. He specified that each type of herb would yield "seed after his kind," and that each tree would yield "fruit, whose seed was in itself" (Genesis 1:11-12). Each did exactly as He commanded: the seed of any plant is within the plant (or the fruit) itself. That seed will produce exactly the same fruit from which it came.

When He created the fish of the sea and the fowl of the air, they also were made to bring forth "after their kind" (Genesis 1:21). Every type of bird reproduces only its own kind and every fish reproduces only itself. Even with mutations, they will not produce other kinds of birds or fish.

When He created all the animals, they were all made to bring forth "after his kind" (Genesis 1:25). They all reproduce after their own kind. They do not even reproduce other related kinds. Your German shepherd will not produce a red fox; your Labrador retriever will not produce a timber wolf.

Their seed is found in themselves. It is easy to understand how we can find the seed of any living thing in itself. The watermelon plant produces the watermelon seed; the giraffes produce more giraffes.

Whether plant or animal, the seed of any particular one of them is found in themselves. So, if you want beans, you must plant bean seeds; if you want corn, you must plant corn seeds.

Again, the natural world is a picture of the spiritual world; the natural order of things is a picture of the spiritual order of things. If we want to see the results of faith, we must plant the seed of faith.

Many want to see the harvest of faith. They want the yield of miracles. They hope and wish and fantasize about it, but they never plant the seed of faith.

They claim to believe in all the power of God, but they never act on it. I could say to everyone that I meet, "I believe in spinach. Everybody should have spinach every day. Everybody should raise spinach in their gardens. It is the cure-all for all of our illnesses. It works wonders for Popeye, and it will work wonders for the rest of us. And besides, the price of spinach is about to rise to such a degree, that it is the best investment you could possibly make at this time."

However, if I do not plant spinach seed, I will never reap a spinach harvest. It will not matter if I have three warehouses full of spinach seed, I will not gain any spinach from it if I do not plant it. As a result, I will never reap the results of spinach for my body, or my wallet.

Many Christians do just that. They believe God can work miracles of healings in their bodies. They believe God can help them to prosper spiritually, physically, and financially. But they never plant any seeds for this to happen. They do not claim the promises of God. They do not release their faith.

"A Bit Much"

Now unto him that is able to do exceedingly abundantly above all that we ask or think, according to the power that worketh in us, Unto him be glory in the church by Christ Jesus throughout all ages, world without end. Amen (Ephesians 3:20-21).

For my thoughts are not your thoughts, neither are your ways my ways, saith the Lord. For as the heavens are higher than the earth, so are my ways higher than your ways, and my thoughts than your thoughts (Isaiah 55:8-9).

I was preaching in Wisconsin where, during the revival, I went to do some visitation with the assistant pastor. We were going to visit a woman who had never attended the church, but whose 12-year-old son had started attending, by way of the Sunday School bus route.

On the way, I began to tell the young minister friend of mine about some of the miracles that had happened in the last series of revival meetings where I had been. One miracle in particular was concerning a woman who, among other things, had difficulty walking because her nerves had died, from her waist down to her feet. She lost all feeling in her legs. But God had healed her.

When we arrived and began speaking with the woman, it turned out that she had the same exact condition as the prior woman. This sparked the faith of the assistant pastor. He told her about what I had just finished telling him in the car. He told her that if she would allow us to pray for her, he believed God would heal her.

She responded by telling us that she was a Lutheran, and that

Lutherans believed in faith. She had great faith. In fact, she was noted for her faith. But to ask God to do this was "a bit much."

He then told her that we were perhaps a little bit different. We believed the Bible, including the passages where it says that nothing is too hard for God (Genesis 18:14; Jeremiah 32:17,27; Mark 10:27). She replied that she too believed that God could do anything but to ask Him to do this was still "a bit much."

I stood back and watched the two interact. He kept trying to convince her that God could, and would, heal her. She kept insisting that it was "a bit much." Well, she won the debate. But she lost her chance for a miracle.

You can have a barn full of corn seed, but if you do not plant it, you will never gain a harvest of corn. You can have a barn full of the seed of faith, but if you do not plant it, you will never reap the harvest that should grow out of faith. You can have all the faith in the world, but if you never use it, it will profit you nothing.

The Seed of God

The Word of God is our seed. In the interpretation of the parable of the sower, Jesus said, "The sower soweth the word" (Mark 4:14). So the Word is our seed.

That word, if it falls on good ground, will produce fruit. What is the fruit that it will produce? Well, the Word of God is, in a crude sense, the seed of God, or the seed of His kingdom. Again, since the word is an extension of the spirit, the Word of God is an "extension" of Himself. So the fruit that it produces will be after His kind. We will become like Him.

The fruit of His seed or His Word is, among other things, the fruit of the Spirit described in Galatians 5:22-23. But even here, what is mentioned (love, joy, peace, etc.) is used to describe characteristics of the fruit of the Spirit. The meaning of the fruit of the Spirit surpasses all of these.

We understand that the natural world teaches us about the spiritual world. All things reproduce "after their own kind." So it is with the Word of God, which is the seed of the kingdom. When we are born of the Spirit, we are born of God. We are born into His kingdom.

Being born of God, we become called the "sons of God" (I John 3:1). Jesus also said that "the good seed are the children of the kingdom" (Matthew 13:38).

Kingdoms have to do with the exercise of authority and power. When we talk about the kingdom of Alexander the Great, we are talking about the area over which he exercised his authority and power. When we talk about the kingdom of Nebuchadnezzar, we are talking about the exercise of his authority and power. Likewise, when we are talking about the kingdom of God, we are talking about the exercise of His authority and power. We are talking about the domain of God.

We can understand how there is not much difference between the bean and the bean seed, or between the corn and the corn seed; it is simply a matter of the different stages of growth. So it is with the seed of the Word: first it is planted in us, and the result of our growth is our becoming children of the kingdom.

The seed of God is in Himself, in His Word. Remember that the seed of every living thing is in itself. That seed will reproduce after His own kind. So His Word will reproduce after His own kind.

Again, it is not that we become gods, as in the "New Age" sense. We are talking about becoming like God in the Christian sense:

> ...*we shall be **like him**; for we shall see him as he is* (I John 3:2, emphasis added).

Remember, there is only one true God who is the Creator of all. And the distinction between Him and all others must never be lost. Yet, His seed will reproduce after His own kind.

Simply stated, the Word of God is the seed of God. So if we want the fruit of God, we must plant the seed of God. If we want the harvest or the results of God (and God is, by definition, supernatural), we must utilize the seed. Paul said,

> *Be not deceived; God is not mocked: for whatsoever a man soweth, that shall he also reap* (Galatians 6:7).

He went on to say that if we sowed to the flesh, we would reap corruption; but if we sowed to the Spirit, we would reap life everlasting (v.8).

So how do you sow spiritual seed? Again, the sower sows the word (Mark 4:14). You sow by what you say. You sow by what comes out of your mouth.

The Success of the Seed

Jesus said, "So is the kingdom of God, as if a man should cast seed into the ground" (Mark 4:26).

In the natural world, you sow your seed into the earth. You plant the seed into the ground. In the spiritual world, you sow your seed into spiritual earth. What is spiritual ground?

When God created man, He made man out of the earth, out of the ground. The difference between man and other creation was that man was the only one made with a soul and spirit. The other creatures reside in the natural world only. Human beings, though, dwell in both the natural and the spiritual worlds.

In the natural world, Jesus said that "the earth bringeth forth fruit of herself; first the blade, then the ear, after that the full corn in the ear" (Mark 4:28). The earth will bring forth plenty of fruit, if one will sow seed into it. So we will bring forth fruit, if we plant seed into our hearts. Plant the seed; get the word into your heart.

The type of ground upon which the seed falls will determine the degree of the harvest's success. Some seeds may fall by the wayside. Others will fall on stony ground. Still others will fall on thorny ground. But some will fall on good ground.

The good ground will bring forth either thirtyfold, sixtyfold, or one hundredfold. The earth will determine to what degree the seed will multiply. The seed determines what will be produced, but the earth determines how productive the crop will be.

As man was made from the earth, so man is the soil of the spirit. The name "Adam" means "earth." The heart of man is the spiritual earth. Whatever type of harvest we want, we can get if we will plant the right seed. The earth will bring forth of herself the harvest (Mark 4:28), if the seed is planted.

Likewise, man, as the spiritual earth, will produce spiritual harvest if we will but plant the seed. This will work whether we plant the seed in ourselves or others.

The type of soil into which the seed falls determines the productiveness of the seed. If we will open ourselves to the seed (which is the Word of God), then we will make it productive in our lives.

Good ground does not usually just appear magically, though, as if it came out of nowhere. It is true that some ground will be finer than others, more suited to growing crops by its very composition: some is purer, richer, darker soil, whereas other soil may be full of sand, clay, shale, rocks, etc.

More often, though, we may have to do something to the soil to get it into a profitable condition, one that will yield results. It may need to be fallowed, or "broken up, harrowed, or plowed without seeding to destroy weeds and conserve soil moisture."[13]

Fallow may also refer to the period of time after the land is tilled, during the growing season.[14] In this time, the soil is allowed to recuperate, or replenish its supply of nutrients. Let us cultivate such fallow ground for the Lord, then, either by plowing it to break up areas of aridity or hardheartedness, or by allowing it to remain still for a while, so that it may be nurtured with refreshing rains and energizing minerals. In due season, it will then be ready to be plowed, and will produce a rich harvest.

> *Humble yourselves therefore under the mighty hand of God, that he may exalt you in due time* [lift you up in due season] (I Peter 5:6).

Samuel told the people of Israel to prepare their hearts unto the Lord (I Samuel 7:3). A prophet told Jehosaphat that there were some good things found in him; namely, that he had prepared his heart to seek God (II Chronicles 19:3). Ezra was able to be used by God because he had:

> *...prepared his heart, to seek the law of the Lord, and to* **do** **it** (Ezra 7:6,10, emphasis added).

Our hearts ought to be prepared beforehand, willing to receive the Lord when He comes. If our house (or soil), is set in order, cleared of confusion, the Master (the sower) can dwell in it (sow the seed, the Word) all the more readily, effectively, and even joyfully—His work will become a pleasure. Does it not feel good to have our house clean, i.e, live in a state of friendship with God?

For the seed to be planted in good ground, we must *hear,* or receive, the Word of God, and obey it fully. Remember, we receive hearing by the Word of God.

> *Faith* [which is what activates God] *cometh by hearing, and hearing by the word of God* (Romans 10:17).

As we physically receive the Word of God, we receive spiritual hearing, which causes us to receive faith. If we harden our hearts to the Word of God, we will be like stony ground, which is unprofitable. If we neglect to focus on it, the cares of this world will choke it out. But if we will mix faith with the Word of God, then it (the seed) becomes profitable to us (Hebrews 4:2).

The seed determines what is produced, but only if it is cast into the ground:

> *Except a corn of wheat fall into the ground and die, it abideth alone: but if it die, it bringeth forth much fruit* (John 12:24).

When Jesus came, He came as the Word made flesh (John 1:14a). He was Life wrapped in a shell of humanity. As the seed made flesh, He was cast into the ground. Man is the earth into which He was cast: He left His throne of glory and dwelt among us (John 1:14b). And that seed died; Jesus died on the cross.

And so the Word of the Lord was fulfilled. The seed fell into the ground and died, bringing forth much fruit. What kind of fruit does it produce? It brings forth more of the same kind of fruit that it is. Paul wrote,

> *For whom he did foreknow, he also did predestinate to be* **conformed to the image of his Son,** *that he might be* **the first-born among many brethren** (Romans 8:29, emphasis added).

In the plan of God, He destined us to be conformed to the very image or likeness of His Son. This plan would make Him the first of many brothers. We become like Him.

The seed of the Word of God was designed to bring forth much fruit. It will be as effective as the rain or snow is in watering the earth (Isaiah 55:10-11). If we will believe the Word of God, it will be profitable to us (Hebrews 4:2). If we will believe, the Word will work effectually (with definite results) in us (I Thessalonians 2:13).

What Are You Sowing?

> *Be not deceived; God is not mocked: for whatsoever a man soweth, that shall he also reap* (Galatians 6:7).

If a farmer does not want to reap corn, he does not plant corn. If he wants to change his harvest from beans to peas, he needs only to change his seed. Likewise, if you do not like the harvest you are reaping, then change the seeds you are sowing.

Learn to speak words of life, not death. Learn to speak words of health rather than sickness. Our words should minister salvation, not condemnation. They should work restoration instead of destruction. Remember you will reap whatever you learn to say with your mouth. The seeds you sow are your words; the words you speak are your seeds.

Discipline your words to be words of success, not failure. Let your words speak wealth and prosperity, rather than poverty and destitution. Learn to look for great rewards, instead of expecting disappointment.

Let your words call for deliverance, instead of bondage. Sow seeds of words that minister freedom, rather than slavery. Speak words of liberty in place of words of captivity. Make your words those of truth, not of error.

Learn to speak of winning rather than losing. Speak of triumphing instead of declining. Instead of murmuring of defeat, let your words be filled with reports of victory!

Speak of rising rather than falling; find words that do not "fall." Talk not of ruin, but of building. Speak words that build up the people of God rather than words that tear them down; let your words edify, not destroy. Choose the side of life: with your words, build up the kingdom. Choose to vivify, create, preserve, establish, raise, amplify, magnify, grow, and produce. Do not use words that ravage, raze, quash, crush, eradicate, annihilate, obliterate, devastate, and demolish. In the things of God, gather, rather than scatter (Luke 11:23).

So, do not discourage, dishearten, or deflate others. Seek to encourage, hearten, embolden, spur, inspire, rally, reassure, root for, fortify, support, buoy, cheer.

Tell others to have confidence, placing trust in God, for "If God is for us, who can stand against us?" (Romans 8:31). God is greater than whatever, or whoever, comes against us.

> *No weapon formed against us shall prosper; and every tongue which rises against you in judgment You shall condemn. This is the heritage of the servants of the Lord, and their righteousness is from Me, says the Lord* (Isaiah 54:17, NKJV).

Nothing "can separate us from the love of Christ" (Romans 8:35-38). We proclaim the love of Christ, and support His cause 100%—not that of the "principalities and powers" of the world which live only for division, to separate believers from God. We should speak what is good or profitable, or nothing at all ("If you have nothing good to say, say nothing at all"). If we cannot do someone good, than we should not do them wrong ("If I can't do you right, I will not do you any wrong").

More than refraining from burdening our neighbors, we are to ease their burdens and encourage them also to say and do what is right:

Now we exhort you, brethren, warn them that are unruly, comfort the feebleminded, support the weak, be patient toward all men. See that none render evil for evil unto any man; but ever follow that which is good, both among yourselves, and to all men. Rejoice evermore. Pray without ceasing. In every thing give thanks: for this is the will of God in Christ Jesus concerning you. Quench not the spirit. Despise not prophesyings (I Thessalonians 5:14-19).

In all things, speak words that do not quench the spirit, but lift it. Prophesy words that work towards edification, exhortation (encouragement), and comfort (I Corinthians 14:3). Let your words speak healings and miracles. Do not let your words be fraught with doubt and unbelief; rather, speak words filled with faith. Learn to speak words that work wonders. Learn to speak the Word of God.

If we do so, we will find our unbelief vanish, and faith will fill the place made by its leaving. In this way we can be filled, more and more, with faith. Instead of being imploded or impaled by our own words, lingering in the shadow of death, we will live by words of faith, in the fullness of life.

Your tongue is the rudder to your ship. It is like the bit to the horse's mouth. Where you go in life depends on what you say.

If you allow your flesh or carnal nature to dictate what you sow, then you will of your flesh reap corruption. You will self-destruct. If instead you allow the Spirit of God to dictate what you sow, you will of the Spirit reap life everlasting. It will produce life on a much higher level. This is life that is "out of this world."

If we want to reap life everlasting, we must sow seeds of life. We must learn to speak the powerful Word of God, for it is life-giving (Hebrews 4:12).

Concerning the words of God, Solomon said that "they are life unto those that find them, and health to all the flesh" (Proverbs 4:22). Yes, His words produce life and health, even to our fleshly bodies. If that is what you want to reap, then start sowing the right type of seeds.

Let us draw near with a true heart in full assurance of faith, having our hearts sprinkled from an evil conscience, and our bodies washed with pure water. Let us hold fast the profession of our faith without wavering; (for he is faithful that promised;) And let us consider one another to provoke unto love and to good works: Not forsaking the assembling of ourselves together, as the manner of some is; but exhorting one another: and so much the more, as ye see the day approaching (Hebrews 10:22-25).

What Are You Preaching?

A friend of mine once told me what a seasoned and successful minister had said to him: that he would get whatever he preached. If he preached the gospel in a weak fashion, he would get weak results; if he preached it powerfully, as the gospel truly is powerful, his results would be powerful.

Right then and there, I made up my mind: if that was the case, then I would preach God as powerfully as I could imagine Him to be. I wanted to get the greatest results I possibly could.

You also will get what you preach; you will get what you speak. If you preach a great falling away, you will reap a great falling away. If you preach that things can only get worse, they will.

If you preach fear, people will live in fear. If you preach trials and tribulations rather than overcoming the world, you will get loads of trials and tribulations. You will get what you preach.

If you preach revival and growth, you will see it. If you preach unity, you will gain unity in the body. If you preach God as a God of miracles, you will receive miracles. If you preach Him as a healer, you will see healings. If you preach God's promise to pour His Spirit out on all flesh, you will see an outpouring of the Holy Ghost.

If you preach Him as a deliverer, you will see deliverances. If you preach Him as a Savior, you will see salvation come. If you preach Him as a restorer of relationships, you will see Him restore relationships.

God will honor your faith. He will not be mocked or discredited. He will give the increase to what you sow, so that you will reap the benefits or the curses, depending on what seed you used. The Bible tells us that "a man shall eat good by the fruit of his mouth" (Proverbs 13:2a).

At this point, some may want to accuse me of being a "word of faith guy." I must tell you that this is far better than being a "word of doubt guy." And I surely do not want to be known as a "word of fear guy;" this is not what God wants for us. Zacharias praised God in his prophesy, saying:

> *That he would grant unto us, that we being delivered out of the hand of our enemies might serve him without fear, in holiness and righteousness before him, all the days of our life* (Luke 1:74-75).

In spite of everything, the apostles were word of faith preachers. Paul referred to "the word of faith, which we preach" (Romans 10:8). If they can be "word of faith men" then I can be a "word of faith man."

Fear ought not stop us from entering the promised land, as it did the children of Israel who were delivered from Egypt. Fear should not prevent us from reigning in the kingdom of God. He told us to fear not, but that He would give us the words to say (Mark 13:11; Luke 12:11). All we need to do is speak His words in faith; He will do the rest.

I want the words that I speak to minister grace to the hearers. I want my words to be useful to edify or build up the Body of Christ. I know that I can be useful in building up the Body of Christ—if I speak words of faith. "Faith is the substance of things hoped for" (Hebrews 11:1). I can build the things I hope for with faith.

Remember, "Be not deceived; God is not mocked: for whatsoever a man soweth, that shall he also reap" (Galatians 6:7). Sow words of faith.

Learn to Speak Words That Do Not Fall

Returning to I Samuel 3:19, we find that as Samuel grew, "The LORD was with him, and did let none of his words fall to the ground." When Samuel spoke a word from God, not once did he ever "miss it." He was always "right on the money." His words had powerful effects. They never fell to the ground, which is contrary to many "prophets" that we have among us now.

It is not that I want to develop an atmosphere of intolerance concerning people trying to be in tune with God and being used by Him. But I do believe that we can get to a point in our walk with God where He will not allow a single word we speak to fall to the ground. The words we speak can become so sure that it would seem as if they came directly from the mouth of God Himself (II Samuel 16:23).

Because we know in part, we prophesy in part (I Corinthians 13:9). We can only prophesy to the degree that we know, or to the degree that we can see. We prophesy according to our knowledge. To the extent that we know God, we can truly prophesy.

That is why Paul prayed, "that I may know Him" (Philippians 3:10). Oh that we may know Him! Perhaps then we would not see so many of our words fall to the ground, and the power of grace thwarted.

If we would know Him as He longs to be known, so many ineffective, idle words would not be spoken; our words would then carry great power, and accomplish great things.

As we grow in grace and in the knowledge of our Lord and Savior Jesus Christ (II Peter 3:18), we will learn to speak His words, which do not fall. In fact, Solomon proclaimed:

> *...There hath not failed one word of of all his good pleasure, which he promised* (I Kings 8:56).

---

[13] *Webster's.* Springfield, Mass: Merriam Webster, Inc., 1996. p.419.

[14] Ibid.

CHAPTER FIFTEEN
THE WHEEL OF NATURE
Our Words Activate Our Nature

And the tongue is a fire, a world of iniquity: so is the tongue among our members, that it defileth the whole body, and setteth of fire the course of nature; and it is set on fire of hell (James 3:6).

James explains that our whole bodies can be defiled by the tongue. Why? It is because it (the tongue) is a medium of the spirit. Is it no wonder that chants—words—are used in witchcraft and seances, as well as in worship and praise to God? If an evil spirit uses the tongue, it can set on fire the course of nature. It will begin the destructive fires of sinful flesh.

James said that our tongue sets on fire "the course of nature." The Greek word for "course" is *trokon*, which refers to a wheel, a course, or a runner. Its meaning encompasses anything that refers to a free, uninhibited progression. Once lit by the fires of hell, the fires keep burning, spiraling out of control. Unless they learn to drink the living water, which alone satisfies (John 4:10,13), such combustible individuals face the likely prospect of participating in eternal combustion.

The word behind "nature" is *geneseos*, which refers to our birth or lineage. This comes from the same word from which we get the words "generations," "genetics," and "genes."

In other words, we are all born with a certain genetic package, which plays a part in determining who we are. But we can activate those genes or limit them, depending on what we say.

James said that the tongue is a fire that "defileth the whole body." Jesus taught us that what truly defiled the man was not what went into the mouth, but what came out of it. James tells us that what comes out of the mouth can defile, not just the soul or spirit of a man, but also the body.

James went on to say that it (the tongue) is what sets on fire the course of nature or the wheel of genetics. He went on to say that human nature was "set on fire of hell," that is, placed under the agitation of evil spirits so as to incite in us lustful or covetous desires of every kind, worshiping and serving the creature rather than the Creator (Romans 1:24-25). That which is "set on fire of hell" works to destroy us, not only spiritually, but also mentally, emotionally, socially, and even physically.

We are just now coming to understand the role that genetics plays in our lives. It affects not only our hair color and height, but can also play a part in our weight, health, and perhaps even our personalities.

Man started out with a perfect genetic sequence. Man was created in the image of God. But sin was introduced, and it corrupted man's nature (Romans 1:23). The course of man's nature, or the wheel of our genetic makeup, was then debased.

As a result, death and disease were introduced to the human race—spiritually, physically, mentally, and emotionally. This does not mean that we human beings are totally without hope. Man has not been totally destroyed—that is what the devil desires to do, but he has not yet accomplished it.

He comes about as a roaring lion seeking whom he may devour (I Peter 5:8). He comes only to steal, to kill, and to destroy (John 10:10a); that is what will happen to us if we allow our corrupted nature to fulfill its lust.

But Jesus said that He came that we might have life, and have it more abundantly (John 10:10b). He came to destroy the works of the devil (I John 3:8). He came to seek and to save that which was lost (Luke 19:10). He came to save even that which has been burned into ashes, as a result of being set on fire of hell (James 3:6). The prophet said that He came to give beauty for ashes (Isaiah 61:3).

Good News Concerning Genetics

The good news (gospel) of Jesus Christ is that He can even change your genetic makeup, in a manner of speaking. (Hear me out on this thought.) He came to save spirit, soul, and body. We know that we will not receive our glorified bodies until He comes again. Nevertheless, Jesus still desires to minister to the whole person. He does not just save souls; He makes men whole. He also heals bodies.

Some people claim today that their problem is in their genetic makeup. Thus, they were born with an uncontrollable sexual drive, or a violent nature. They were born with a hot temper because of their nationality. Genetic makeup is supposedly responsible for the propensity in some toward addiction to drugs, alcohol, or cigarettes. Some point to their genes, trying to lay the blame on them for their weakness toward gambling. They point to the course of nature. They try to blame the wheel of genetics. They say they were born with a deviant sexual lust, such as homosexuality, or the perverted urge to be a pedophile. They say they inherited a certain weakness from their parents.

At this point, I am not arguing whether or not it is so. What matters is that Jesus came to set the captives free, in every aspect of their being. He was sent:

> ...to heal the brokenhearted, to preach deliverance to the captives, and recovering of sight to the blind, to set at liberty them that are bruised (Luke 4:18).

Regardless of what you have heard about any of your problems or weaknesses (that they are supposedly the result of poor genetic make-up), there is power in the Holy Ghost able to transform you. It can actually change your nature. Old things will pass away, and all things will become new (II Corinthians 5:17). The kingdom of God possesses the power to change, and transform, YOU. There truly is wonder-working power in the blood of the Lamb.

> How much more shall the blood of Christ, who through the eternal Spirit offered himself to God without spot to God, purge your conscience from dead works to serve the living God? (Hebrews 9:14, NKJV).

Remember, we are able to overcome by the blood of the Lamb and by the word of our testimony (Revelation 12:11). The blood of the Lamb has already been shed; what is left is for you to speak out the word of your testimony. Claim the power of the blood of Jesus. Truly, that blood will reach the highest mountain, and flow to the lowest valley. And that blood will never lose its power.

The blood of Jesus cleanses us from all of our sins (I John 1:7). As one songwriter said, "Would you be free from the burden of sin? Would you be free from your passion and pride? Would you be whiter, much whiter, than snow? There is wonder-working power in the blood." If we would be free of whatever ails us, we simply need to humbly implore His strength, and obey the Word He speaks to our hearts:

> Therefore lay aside all filthiness and overflow of wickedness, and receive with meekness the implanted word, which is able to save your souls (James 1:21, NKJV).

Why Fight Against Yourself?

Jesus taught that a house, or a kingdom, divided against itself cannot stand (Mark 3:24-25). In the same way, we will not be able to stand if we are divided against ourselves. If I am fighting against myself, my enemy does not need to worry about me, for I will be an easy prey for him.

Paul shows us that we are our own worst enemies when we fight against ourselves. But he also pinpoints the way out of the traps of our own making. In meekness, we are to instruct:

> ...*those that oppose themselves; if God peradventure will give them repentance unto the acknowledging of the truth; And that they may recover themselves out of the snare of the* devil, **who are taken captive by him at his will** (II Timothy 2:25-26, emphasis added).

I have encountered numerous individuals who have trouble living for God, just because they are always warring against themselves. Divided—fragmented and alienated—against themselves, they cannot stand ("Divided we fall; united we stand").

I have also met many pastors, who sincerely love the Lord and are trying to experience revival and growth, but they are frustrated that they never seem to accomplish much. They take five steps forward, and four and a half steps back. They think the devil is fighting them, when in reality, they are simply "shooting themselves in the foot."

How is it that we unwittingly oppose ourselves? How do we fight against ourselves, without even realizing it? Scripture teaches us that the weapons of our warfare are not carnal (fleshly). Rather, our weapons include (but are not limited to): the **Word** of God, the sword of the Spirit; the word of our testimony (Revelation 12:11), by which, combined with the blood of Jesus, we overcome the enemy; and prayer, praise, and words of faith or deliverance. In many cases, **our words are an essential part of our weaponry**.

Even though our weapons are not physical, they are nonetheless (and even more) powerful—effectual, result-producing—through God to the pulling down of strongholds,

> *Casting down imaginations, and every high thing that exalteth itself against the knowledge of God, and bringing into captivity every thought to the obedience of Christ* (II Corinthians 10:4-5).

So our words must be made to wage war for us, not against us. In the well-known children's story of "the little engine that could," the engine used his mouth to encourage and strengthen himself so that he could make it to the top of the mountain. Likewise, we are to make our words enable and empower us and those around us.

But not only must our words work for us, our thoughts must do so as well. Paul told the Philippian Church that they were to harness their thoughts towards certain things:

> *Finally, brethren, whatsoever things* are *true, whatsoever things are honest, whatsoever things* are *just, whatsoever things* are *pure, whatsoever things* are *lovely, whatsoever things* are *of good report; if* there be *any virtue, and* there be *any praise, think on these things* (Philippians 4:8).

The next verse in Philippians states that if we would do these things, the God of peace would be with us. Then we would not be bound by fear, but would have a peace that passes understanding (v.7), and our words would minister that peace (rather than tormenting fear) to those who hear us. Our words will express the abundance of peace in our spirit, which is gathered in our thoughts.

Why Speak Your Destruction?

Proverbs 18:7 says, "A fool's mouth is his destruction, and his lips are the snare of his soul." Notice that it did not say that a "wicked man's" mouth was his own destruction; we would not doubt that. It said a "fool's" mouth is his destruction.

According to the Scriptures, the way in which some Christians live their lives would classify them as foolish. More specifically, the way some Christians "run their mouths" classifies them as foolish. The fool will use the power of his own words to destroy himself.

Some people today do the same thing. They say: "I think I am getting cancer"; "I think I am coming down with the flu"; "I believe I will fail this test"; "I think I will be rejected for this job"; and, "Things are bad for me now, and they are going to get worse." If they plant those seeds, they will reap that harvest.

Some will use their tongue to "set on fire the course of nature." They claim a weakness in health because of genetics; they will be sure to get it.

They plant seeds of their own destruction. It should come as no surprise that they reap a similar harvest. An uncontrolled tongue will activate the course of nature that is set on fire of hell. They will, of the flesh, reap corruption.

They say, "My father was an alcoholic, so I will be one. My mother abused drugs; that means I will, too. I will never gain victory over this lust; I will never conquer this problem; I was born this way—I cannot change."

> Be not deceived; God is not mocked: for whatsoever a man soweth, that shall he also reap (Galatians 6:7).

If you sow seeds to the flesh, you will reap corruption. Do not sow those seeds; sow to the Spirit by speaking the Word of God.

Jesus said, "Be of good cheer; I have overcome the world" (John 16:33). The apostle John wrote, "Greater is he that is in you, than he that is in the world" (I John 4:4). We can overcome the world if the Holy Ghost is in us. He is greater than he that is in the world.

He also said, "Whatsoever is born of God overcometh the world" (I John 5:4). If we are born of God, if we are born of the Spirit (John 3:5; Acts 2:4), we can enter into the kingdom of God and overcome the world.

Paul talked about those that would not inherit the kingdom of God. He said that among these were the fornicators, idolaters, the adulterers, the effeminate, the abusers of themselves with mankind (homosexuals), thieves, covetous or greedy people, drunkards, revilers, and extortioners (I Corinthians 6:9-10). But He did not say that, if you were ever in any one of these categories, there was no hope for you. He said:

> And such were some of you: but ye are washed, but ye are sanctified, but ye are justified in the name of the Lord Jesus, and by the Spirit of our God (I Corinthians 6:11).

There is hope for you, if you will take on the name of Jesus (Acts 2:38; 19:5), and be filled with His Spirit.

Others sow seeds of failure and disappointment, ruin and loss; they plant seeds of trouble. In essence, these people are true converts to Murphy's Law; they fully subscribe to the theory that says, "Everything that can go wrong, will go wrong, and at the worst possible moment." Sometimes, they even add their own negative prophecies to the theory. But the last time I checked, that saying was not in the Word of God. That report is from the enemy.

The report of the Lord says that "all things work together for good to them that love God, to them who are the called according to his purpose" (Romans 8:28). The report of the Lord tells me that, as long as I am called according to His purpose and love God, then everything is going to work out for my good. It does not matter what may go wrong, it will still work out right for me. What a promise to stand on!

Whose Report Do You Believe?

In Romans 10:8, the Word is called a word of faith. Notice that it is not called a word of doubt. When you speak the Word of God, you are speaking the word of faith. The seeds you are planting are seeds of faith.

His Word is not a word of doubt or unbelief; neither is it called a word of fear. The Scriptures talk about the faith of God, but they do not talk about the doubt of God.

Scripture does talk about a fear of God, but this refers to a reverence and respect of His power, His ways, and His person. The Bible refers to "the fear of the Lord," not as a tormenting fear, but as one that brings out a healthy respect for the holiness of the Lord.

God Himself does not seek to terrify us with a fear that tortures us. But He would like us to be awed by who He is, so that we would cry out, like the four living creatures before His throne,

Holy, holy, holy is the Lord God Almighty, who was, who is and is to come (Revelation 4:8).

We should never cease worshipping Him who sits on the throne for ever and ever, giving Him "glory, honor and thanks" (Revelation 4:9-10). When we speak the word of God, it should come out of a pure heart, full from worshipping the Lord, giving Him all the glory. It is the word of faith, and it should therefore reflect the Spirit from which it comes.

Contrary to the thinking of some, it is not a word of fear. It is neither a word of pain and suffering, nor a word of loss and defeat. For God is positive—He always works to a positive result—even if He has to use a negative to get there.

We need to be full of the Word of God. We must strive to be full of faith, which surmounts all difficulties.

Some folks I know seem to work hard at being full of unbelief. It appears that they have been doused with doubt; it looks as if they are ruled by fear. They are drenched in unbelief, covered in negativity. As a result, they become insulated to the words of faith God is speaking to their hearts. (God may say to you at a critical moment, "Trust that I am able to take care of you," or in a time of blessing, "See, your Father knows how to give you good gifts.") Thus, without receiving these words of encouragement which God wants to give them, faith is rarely, if ever, activated in their lives.

They seem to be willing to believe anything but the word of God. They can believe the doctor's report, but not the report of the Lord. They take the word of the secular psychologist over the word of the Lord. They believe the sayings of the media, or some "expert," but they disregard the word of God.

You may even show them a Scripture that contradicts the "experts," and one that contains the answer they need. They respond to the Scripture by saying, "Yes, I know the Bible says that, but you do not understand."

They are more willing to believe the enemies' lies than to believe the promises of God. They may hear preaching, but they never allow it to become a part of them, a part of their spirit; it never gets into their spirit. It does not enter into their heart, and so does not become a part of their thinking. They never mix or mingle the promises of God with faith.

Learn to make the Word of God so much a part of your life that it becomes engrafted into your spirit, so that you rely on the words He is speaking to you. Remember, it is the engrafted word which is able to save us (James 1:21).

CHAPTER SIXTEEN
RELEASING YOUR FAITH
Garnering the Power of Your Spirit

Hebrews 1:3 says that God is upholding all things by the "word of his power." It did not say that all things were upheld by the power of God's Word, but rather by the word of His power.

God activates His power by His word. All things are upheld by the word of His power. So we also activate the power of our spirit, by our words.

Hebrews 11:1 says that "faith is the substance of things hoped for, the evidence of things not seen." Now we know that faith is a spiritual substance, not a physical one. It is found in the spiritual world.

Therefore to release faith, our spirit man must be involved. It is not simply a matter of speaking a word physically, although that is a start. If the power of the spirit is to be released, the spirit must be speaking the word.

It is not a matter of just saying the right words, though this is better than saying the wrong words. But to activate the faith of God, it must come from your spirit being free from the weights that hinder your will and desire. If you will speak the Word of God from your spirit (your innermost being), then the power of the Word of God can be released.

If all you can do is simply speak the right words, then say them "until it gets into your spirit." Once it—the message, the concept, or the *faith* behind the words—gets into your spirit, the word will have great effect, calling down the power of God to do what the words say. Jesus said,

> *Whosoever shall say unto this mountain, Be thou removed, and be thou cast into the sea; and shall not doubt in his heart, but shall believe that those things which he saith shall come to pass; he shall have whatsoever he saith* (Mark 11:23).

Jesus told us that the moving of the mountain was based on speaking the word to that mountain with the faith of God. But when we speak to the mountain, it must come from the heart, the spirit.

The spirit must be in agreement with what we say. Otherwise, there is doubt in the heart.

For your spirit to be involved in sending out the Word of God, it is similar to the power of an engine being "gathered together" in one block: if the engine block is cracked or broken, you will get no use from the power that otherwise would have been available from that engine. You must garner all the power of the engine into one place.

In a sense, this is how it is with the operation of faith. You must garner the power of your spirit. Garnering the power of your spirit or your will is accomplished by setting your will free from distractions. You must lay aside every weight that would so easily beset you in this race we are running.

Laying Aside the Weights Equals Setting Your Spirit Free

In the legends of King Arthur and the knights of his round table, one of the greatest knights was Sir Galahad, who was counted worthy to drink from the Holy Grail. It is recorded that Sir Galahad made the statement, "My strength is as the strength of ten because my heart is pure." Because he lived a pure life, his will and power were free from weights that would have otherwise weighed him down.

Athletes do not perform as well when they have their conscience riddled with guilt or worry. Workers do not work as well when there are problems in the home. Accidents often happen when someone "has their mind elsewhere," for whatever reason. We must be totally focused in order to gain the aid of the power of our spirit. Only through purity can our spirit work unhindered. Purity helps release the power residing in our spirit.

Distractions especially include worry, fear, and guilt from sin. If any of these is on your mind, it will be difficult to garner your spirit to agree with you concerning a matter. This is where receiving the Word of God helps: the more you hear it, say it, and obey it, the more you will receive spiritual hearing, and thus cause weights to be released from your spirit.

The more you can hear God's voice, the less distractions will bother you (and the less the evil spirits will succeed in afflicting you). Remember that, if the devil cannot stop you from doing something God would like you to do, he can attempt to harass you with agitating spirits which seek to give you no rest, so that you do not enjoy or even remember what it was you were about.

Thus we lose the fruit of prayer, or do not experience His presence as clearly. In such a distracted state of mind, we cannot minister efficiently. If we are so caught off guard defensively, we cannot advance in the power of the Spirit.

Jesus described certain things that could choke out the seed of the kingdom in us. In Mark 4:19, He said that it could be the cares of this world. This does not have to be something bad: oftentimes it is something good, such as working for a living, a pet project we may have, or going to contests in which our children are participating. Each of these may be a good thing, but it should not get in the way of the kingdom of God.

I know of one minister and his wife who lost out on their ministry because they put the attending of 4-H meetings as a higher priority. This activity may have been good, but placing it higher than the kingdom of God on the priority list choked out their seed.

Some have choked out the seed of the kingdom in their lives with the thorns of the "obligations of work." Others have lost out with God while "trying to get an education." Still others have had their seeds choked out by getting involved in political or social activities. Again, none of these things are wrong in themselves. Usually, they are even beneficial. But they must not be done obsessively, to the detriment of the coming of the kingdom of God.

Jesus also mentioned the deceitfulness of riches as being able to choke out the seed of the kingdom. I know of many who never desired to leave God, but their seed was choked out because of their pursuit of riches. Do not get me wrong—I believe God wants His children to prosper. But I know of many who pursued great riches, "temporarily," so that, in the end, they could do all these great things for God with the money they had earned. In the end, they never did see the kingdom of God bring their "fruit to perfection" (Luke 8:14), because thorns had choked out their seed.

Jesus also talked about the lusts of other things that could enter in and choke the seed. This could refer to desires of any kind that seek only to gratify the flesh. Luke 8:14 refers to these as the "pleasures of this life." I know of many who lost out with God because they took too many hunting or fishing trips on the weekend, and thus missed church so often, that they grew weak spiritually.

The distractions do not have to be among the things that I have mentioned as examples: it could be anything that is not necessarily wrong, and even is good. But we ought not to let the good get in the way of the best. There is a season for everything (Ecclesiastes 3:1)— not just "hunting season," "shopping season," "planting season," "football season," "fishing season," "baseball season," etc.

There is a time for every purpose, and a little moderation will not harm us. However, we must guard against letting our life become a series of overlapping seasons, from which we seldom, if ever, take a break. Others more rightly deserve the priority of our attention: God, our family, and so on.

When your spirit is frayed and distracted, behind every word of faith that you speak will be a seed of doubt, that will nag the back resources of your mind. This power drain makes it difficult to exercise the faith of God. This is why we cannot live in what we understand to be sin, and still see the great power of God manifested. Those weights of guilt fetter our faith and shackle our spirit. We are made incapable of ministering to others, or even saving ourselves.

We do need diversion, recreation of spirit and body, or a "change of pace." The only caution we need is that excesses can lead us to be caught unawares, unprepared.

Webster's Dictionary defines *unawares* as "without design, attention, preparation, or premeditation," or, "without warning: suddenly, unexpectedly."[15] Our awareness level must be raised so that we are conscious of the things that are important to God. If we are caught unprepared, Matthew tells us how the Lord will respond:

> But if and that evil servant shall say in his heart, My lord delayeth his coming; and shall begin to smite his fellow-servants, and to eat and drink with the drunken; The lord of that servant shall come in a day when he looketh not for him, and in an hour that he is not aware of, and shall cut him asunder, and appoint him his portion with the hypocrites: there shall be weeping and gnashing of teeth (Matthew 24:48-51).

The Lord's intention in speaking the preceding message was not to frighten, but to show that there are sobering consequences to slothfulness. But Jesus does not stop with the affirmation of His justice. He emphasizes the spirit of the law, which points out the positive aspect of His commandments: not only are we *not* to do certain things, we *are* to live out the corresponding virtues which are implied. For example, the commandment not to commit adultery means that we should love our

143

spouses as God loves us. Instead of saying, "do this or die," Jesus wants to encourage his disciples, saying, "do this and *live*." How much does God desire to bless our faithfulness!

> *Who then is a faithful and wise servant, whom his lord hath made ruler over his household, to give them meat in due season? Blessed is that servant, whom his lord when he cometh shall find so doing. Verily I say unto you, That he shall make him ruler over all his goods* (Matthew 24:45-47).

We ought to season everything we do with salt, or fire, to keep our focus freshened and our relationships renewed:

> *For everyone will be seasoned with fire, and every sacrifice will be seasoned with salt. Salt is good, but if the salt loses its flavor, how will you season it? Have salt in yourselves, and have peace with one another* (Mark 9:49).

In this way, we will avoid the pitfall of suddenly finding ourselves in the valley, knowing not how we arrived there. So let us stay on the narrow path, bridle in mouth, so to speak, led by the Master (Proverbs 3:5-6). We must jealously protect, and zealously nourish our seed, to let the plant of the kingdom of God flourish in our gardens, and keep the flame of faith alive within us:

> *Therefore I remind you to stir up* [fan into flame] *the gift of God which is in you* (II Timothy 1:6).

Focused Asking

We desire to receive some things from God. But sometimes it would be more accurate to say that we fantasize about receiving certain desires from Him, then wonder why we never obtain them. James wrote that part of our problem is our neglecting to ask of God. "Ye have not, because ye ask not" (James 4:2).

Yet, our asking must not be from a heart that is trying to serve two masters. We must not be asking for things to serve our fleshly nature. "Ye ask, and receive not, because ye ask amiss, that ye may consume it upon your lusts" (James 4:3).

We cannot be focused on two different worlds. If we ask, we must ask out of a pure heart, for it is the pure (singly focused) in heart that shall see God in manifestation (Matthew 5:8).

When we ask, we must not be double-minded, or we are not going to receive any request from God. Concerning one who is wavering in the sincerity, or purity, of his desire towards God (i.e., his faith), James wrote,

> Let not that man think that he shall receive any thing of the Lord (James 1:7).

We Speak It First

In Genesis 1, we find that before God performed any of His creative acts, He usually spoke a word. He will tell of a thing before He brings it to pass.

> Remember the former things of old: for I am God, and there is none else; I am God, and there is none like me. Declaring the end from the beginning, and from ancient times the things that are not yet done, saying, My counsel shall stand, and I will do all my pleasure...Yea, I have spoken it, I will also bring it to pass; I have purposed it, I will also do it (Isaiah 46:9-11).

> I have even from the beginning declared it to thee; before it came to pass I shewed it thee (Isaiah 48:5).

Man was created in the image of God: the image (form, pattern, blueprint, thought, or word) of God preceded the actual creation of physical and spiritual substance. As God speaks a word before it is accomplished, so, in the same way, we speak a word, usually aloud, before we perform a thing. We say: "I am going to change the oil in my car"; "I am going to the office"; "I will get a degree from college"; "I will build my dream house"; "I will finish this project"; and, "Let us eat supper."

In a sense, we were designed to work this way, with a plan that we must first, or soon, communicate. In fact, it can be difficult for us to work on a project without telling a single soul about it. At the very least, we will talk to ourselves about it.

In speaking it out, we are releasing a word of faith. Then, in order for that faith not to be dead, we back it up with our works or deeds (James 2:26). We act on that faith to see the desired result.

On numerous occasions, God has used Brother Billy Cole to see at least 3,000 people receive the Holy Ghost in one day. During some of his crusades, he has seen 10,000; 30,000; 40,000; 65,000; and 78,000 receive the Holy Ghost in one day. But in his experience, it has not always been that way.

Long before any of this happened, he would see 25, 50, and maybe even over 100 receive the Holy Ghost in one service. But he would proclaim that he would one day see a "day of Pentecost" where at least 3,000 would receive the gift of the Holy Ghost in one day.

Some skeptics would question him at times saying, "Have you seen it happen yet?" Billy Cole would respond, "No, but I will." He spoke the word of faith first; he sowed the seed of faith for it. Now, he is reaping the harvest of that faith.

Today, Ethiopia is in the middle of what many church leaders have called "the greatest revival in the history of the church." In 25 years, the number of Ethiopians who have been filled with the precious gift of the Holy Ghost has increased from nothing to over one million souls, and the majority of this outpouring has been in the last 10 years.

Ethiopians have seen miracles of every sort. If it is mentioned in the Bible, they have seen it. They have seen the blinded eyes opened, the deaf ears unstopped, the dumb talking, and the lame walking. They have seen lepers cleansed, devils cast out, and numerous people raised from the dead. They have had supernatural visitations of every kind, with Brother Teklemiriam as their leader.

But there have been days of tribulation and violent persecution from the government, various rebel factions, the Muslims, and various "Christian" church organizations (and some persecution still persists today). In those days, there was a promise that the Wendells (the founders of the work), Brother Teklemiriam, and the church would pray and proclaim.

That promise was based on Psalm 68:31 which says, "Ethiopia shall soon stretch out her hands unto God." They prayed it. They proclaimed it. They encouraged each other with it. They ate it. They drank it. They slept it. They breathed it. Most importantly, they believed it. And today they are seeing it happen.

Speaking a word is not all you have to do. The evidence of the faith must be there as well. Faith without works is simply a carcass. So you must do more than simply speak a word.

Herein lies the beginnings of faith; this is the place where the key to the kingdom is found: words spoken in the faith of God, garnering the power of the entire spirit, so that it freely flows, with the graceful agility of the Holy Ghost, into actions which build the kingdom. So never let anybody talk you into the idea that the spoken word is not important: there is tremendous power in a vocalized word (even their attempt at persuasion proves it).

It Is Not Too Difficult to Get Started

In Deuteronomy chapter thirty, God promised the people of Israel certain blessings. In verse nine, He said,

> *The LORD thy God will make thee plenteous in every work of thine hand, in the fruit of thy body, and in the fruit of thy cattle, and in the fruit of thy land.*

Then He says,

> *This commandment which I command thee this day* [the commands necessary to be obeyed in order to receive the blessings that He had promised them], *it is not hidden from thee, neither is it afar off* [in other words, it is not so difficult for you that you are unable to fulfill it; it is not beyond your abilities to access it]. *It is not in heaven, that thou shouldest say, Who shall go up for us to heaven, and bring it unto us, that we may hear it, and do it? Neither is it beyond the sea, that thou shouldest say, "Who shall go over the sea for us, and bring it unto us, that we may hear it, and do it?' But* **the word is very nigh unto thee, in thy mouth, and in thy heart,** *that thou mayest do it"* (Deuteronomy 30:11-14, emphasis added).

To obey the commands of God is not out of reach for us. To do the works of God is not too far removed from us that we cannot attain it. The key to the kingdom is not beyond us. We do not have to wonder if we have the ability to fulfill it. He said that it was extremely simple: the word comes from our mouth, out of our heart (spirit). Reigning in the Spirit begins with speaking the right word from a right spirit. The action of the Spirit continues when we obey to act in faith what He has spoken to our spirit.

Is it really that simple? James compared our tongue to the bit in the horse's mouth and the rudder of a ship. If we will turn our attention to saying the right things, and doing them from the heart, sooner or later our spirit will line up rightly with the Word of the Lord.

Prayer is helpful in this effort. Pray prayers of faith and you soon will be exercising faith. Pray prayers that line up with the perfect will of God, and you soon will line up with the perfect will of God. Pray prayers of righteousness and holiness, and you soon will be living accordingly. The reverse is also true. Paul said, "Evil communications corrupt good manners" (I Corinthians 15:33). He also said,

> Let no corrupt communication proceed out of your mouth, but that which is good to the use of edifying, that it may minister grace unto the hearers (Ephesians 4:29).

If we learn to speak only what is good (and Psalm 34:8 says, "O taste and see that the LORD is good"), we would minister grace to hearers. We know that grace is the influence of God working in us, both to will (desire to do), and also to do, of His good pleasure (Philippians 2:13). The grace of God provides us help in time of need (Hebrews 4:16). It gives us power to live the overcoming life.

The key to the kingdom starts in our mouth. The words we speak are important to our entrance into the kingdom of God. If only we would just speak the right words! If only we would use the Word of God with our mouths, then it would minister grace to the hearers. And one of the first hearers of everything we say is our own self; we hear all the words we say. So we would be ministering that grace to ourselves.

If we would speak the right words, if we would speak the Word of God, then it would unleash the grace of God to work in our lives. Then would His perfect will and good pleasure be performed in our lives, rather than the will of our enemies, who desire our destruction.

In order to live so as to please God, we need a clean heart and a steadfast spirit to be renewed within us, so that we can continually abide in the Lord's presence, full of His Holy Spirit. Let us trust God who is able to inwardly cleanse us so that we may outwardly radiate His light. Jesus our redeemer will help us to be faithful to His will. Let us pray with David:

> Create in me a clean heart, O God; and renew a right spirit within me. Cast me not away from thy presence; and take not thy holy spirit from me (Psalm 51:10-11).

> Let the words of my mouth, and the meditation of my heart, be acceptable in thy sight, O LORD, my strength, and my redeemer (Psalm 19:14).

It is not too difficult to speak the words of the Lord, if we will learn from Him (Matthew 11:29). Paul related how easy it is to speak His words. In writing to the church in Rome, he quoted the book of Deuteronomy:

But what saith it? "The word is nigh thee, even in thy mouth, and in thy heart:" that is, the word of faith, which we preach (Romans 10:8; Deuteronomy 30:14).

Paul called that word, "the word of faith." We must start speaking words of faith. "Lord, even now, let thy kingdom come."

You Have a Choice

After telling the people of Israel that the word was as simple as being in their mouths, God gave them a choice to make. He said, "See, I have set before thee this day life and good, and death and evil" (Deuteronomy 30:15). They had a choice between life and death, based on the word in their mouth.

In Deuteronomy 30:19, He said their choice was between "life and death, blessing and cursing." But it all started with the words they spoke. God then exhorted them to choose life.

The Bible clearly teaches us "that God is no respecter of persons" (Acts 10:34). What principles He may lay down for one, will also work for another.

So I exhort you to encourage and foster life, rather than death; to desire blessing rather than cursing; and to embrace the promises of God, rather than the lies of the enemy.

Choose to reign in the spirit. Decide to begin exercising power and authority in the kingdom of God. Pursue the works that are evidence of a son of God. Take the key to the kingdom, open the door to the supernatural realm, and begin your reign in the spirit.

[15]*Merriam Webster's Collegiate Dictionary*, p. 1284.

Dear Fellow Christian,

I hope this book has enlightened and inspired you to begin your reign as a son of God. If you would like to respond in any way, contact the author concerning speaking engagements, or order any other materials, direct your correspondence to:

Spirit of Life Ministries
4830 Morwanda Dr.
Roanoke, VA 24017-4267.

For a copy of *Power to Tread on Serpents*, enclose payment of $7.00 plus $1.50 shipping and handling per book.

—David Sanzo